BUILDING THE EAST RIDING

BUILDING THE EAST RIDING

A Guide to its Architecture and History

Lynn F Pearson

Smith Settle

First published in 1995 by
Smith Settle Ltd
Ilkley Road
Otley
West Yorkshire
LS21 3JP

ISBN   Paperback   1 85825 030 7
       Hardback   1 85825 031 5

British Library Cataloguing-in-Publication data:
A catalogue record for this book is available from the British Library.

Half-title page: Walmgate Bar, York.
Title page: A door canopy at Jacob's Well, York.

Designed, printed and bound by
SMITH SETTLE
Ilkley Road, Otley, West Yorkshire LS21 3JP

COT
7/95

Contents

Acknowledgements

The publishers and author would like to thank the following for permission to reproduce the illustrations listed below:

Burton Constable Foundation, p130; City of York, p2; Chris Metcalfe, p119; Jim Perry, p21; Shepherd Construction Ltd, pp24, 25; Ken Trethewey, p139; Withernsea Lighthouse Museum Trust, p135; Yorkshire Water Museum, p116.

The line drawings are by Trevor Mitchell. All other illustrations were supplied by the author.

Preface

I T WAS by no means my first experience of the East Riding, but walking the Wolds Way — back to front, as it happened, from Filey to the Humber — where I was enfolded in wolds, far from the everyday world and deep in the quietest countryside, brought home to me the unique qualities of this almost undiscovered Riding. Its architecture ranges from obscure follies and faraway lighthouses, to the grandest of country houses, an incomparable church and a huge, modern bridge. A fine mixture, then; the East Riding is not to be underestimated.

In this book I have tried to provide a guide to the best architecture of the Riding, and following Pevsner's example in his *Buildings of England* series, have also included the City of York; a crowded counterbalance to the empty landscape of Holderness.

Not all of Yorkshire's architecturally interesting buildings are accessible to the public, but that is no reason for omitting such sites from a book which tries to relate the story of the county's architects and architecture. Please remember, then, that access may be non-existent or strictly limited, and respect the privacy of others.

Fortunately, buildings in the care of English Heritage (Burton Agnes Manor House, Clifford's Tower, Kirkham Priory, Skipsea Castle, and Wharram Percy Church and Deserted Medieval Village) and the National Trust (Maister House and Treasurer's House) are open at the times given in the respective handbooks, and many other houses and gardens are open independently.

Many people helped me in my exploration of Yorkshire's least-discovered Riding, and I should like to thank the following for their assistance and advice (although, as ever, any errors and omissions are entirely my own work): Joyce Cockerill for her suggestions regarding the tiles of York, Trevor Ermel of Monochrome for his elegant prints, Chris Metcalfe for advice on the pubs of Hull, the invaluable dog-sitters Jim and Margaret Perry, and Mark Whyman for information on the buildings of Beverley. And not forgetting Sue Hudson and those excellent dogs Boots, Benson and Socks, keen walkers all.

For their generous provision of advice on the historic buildings in their particular areas, I should like to thank the following: the Chief Planning Officer at Beverley Borough Council, Chief Planning and Development Officer at Boothferry Borough Council, Director of Planning and Technical Services at East Yorkshire Borough Council, Director of Development at Holderness Borough Council, Director of Planning and Design at Hull City

Council, Chief Planning Officer at Ryedale District Council, Director of Technical Services at Scarborough Borough Council, Conservation Officer at Selby District Council, and the Directorate of Development Services at the City of York.

I am grateful to the following for their courtesy in granting permission to reproduce illustrations: Burton Constable Foundation, Chris Metcalfe, Jim Perry, Shepherd Construction Ltd, Ken Trethewey, Withernsea Lighthouse Museum Trust and the Yorkshire Water Museum. Trevor Mitchell has once again drawn some excellent illustrations.

This is the final book in the *Building the Ridings* series, and as a runner of half-marathons — best enjoyed after the event — I can safely say that although the writing may have been of marathon length, the enjoyment has been constant throughout. I have discovered building after building which has excited and intrigued me, have found new personal favourites and met buildings which I had only seen in print. I might even take the Wainhouse Tower at Halifax as my luxury item on *Desert Island Discs*! I hope that readers' pleasure in exploring this vast county is as great as mine has been, and continues to be.

Lynn F Pearson
Gosforth, Newcastle upon Tyne
1995

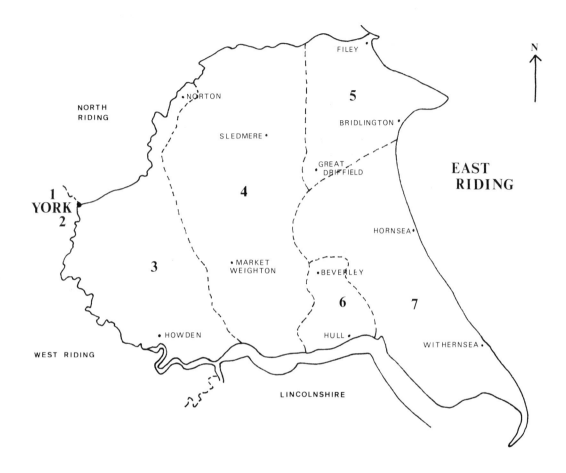

THE WALLED CITY

York within the Walls

TWO AND three-quarter miles. Not a great or particularly significant distance, but a momentous journey: walk the walls of York to see a matchless display of medieval architecture, from castle and Minster to guildhall and parish church. There are Roman remains too, and polite Georgian buildings, but the Industrial Revolution happened elsewhere, leaving the essence of the city firmly medieval.

York's first walls were earthworks, built by the Roman garrison stationed on a site just east of the Ouse from AD 71; their settlement was known as Eboracum, the place of the yews. From the early second century it was defended by a stone wall, and in the generally peaceful period up to the fourth century the town thrived, reaching a population of around 5,000. After the Roman withdrawal in about AD 407, York fell to the Angles, then was captured by the Danes in AD 866 and became their capital, Jorvik. The Normans arrived in the eleventh century to find a successful trading centre; the outer defences of their castle,

begun in 1068, provided the basis for the present city walls.

The city suffered serious fires in 1069 and 1137, but recovered to become an important local and provincial administrative centre, as well as a regional market, during the twelfth and thirteenth centuries. Economic growth continued during the fourteenth century, while the population grew to around 14,000 by its end, despite the coming of the Black Death in 1349 (and four further outbreaks before 1380).

By the late fourteenth century the city had become the most important market centre in the north of Britain; thanks to its position on the River Ouse, North Sea shipping could reach the city's wharfs via the Humber Estuary. Commerce, trade and crafts all flourished: leatherwork, stained glass, stonemasonry and especially textiles in the latter part of the fourteenth century.

But the fourteenth century turned out to be the apogee of the city's prosperity. By the end of the fifteenth century the population had

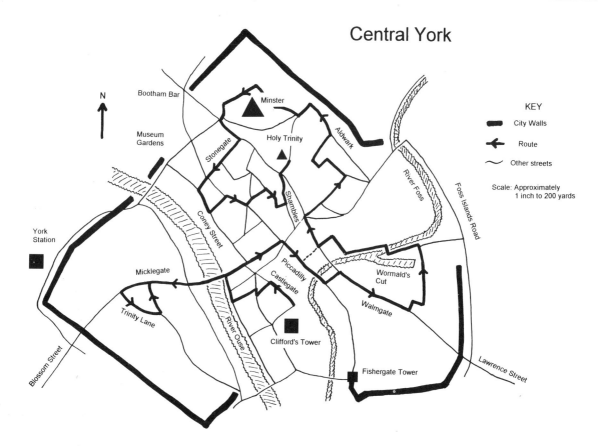

Central York

KEY

City Walls

Route

Other streets

Scale: Approximately
1 inch to 200 yards

N

Bootham Bar

Museum Gardens

Minster

Holy Trinity

Stonegate

Aldwark

River Foss

Foss Islands Road

York Station

Coney Street

Shambles

Micklegate

Castlegate

Piccadilly

Wormald's Cut

Walmgate

Trinity Lane

River Ouse

Clifford's Tower

Fishergate Tower

Lawrence Street

Blossom Street

dropped to around 7,000 and some buildings were in a state of decay. Local industries, particularly textiles, were hit by outside, even foreign, competition; the rise of the West Riding textile industry, with its easy access to water power, hastened the end of York's own textile production. However, the diverse pattern of trading — everything from wine and wool to tar and tin — helped to protect the income of the city's merchants.

The slow decline was arrested by the late seventeenth century, when York once more became fashionable. During the eighteenth century, while mansions were erected on the vast agricultural estates in the surrounding vale, corresponding town houses arose in the city, and Georgian terraces crept along roads outside the walls. York was a social centre with buildings to match.

But without coalmines or sufficient water power, there was no heavy industry on the scale of the West Riding, although iron-founding, glass and chemicals were all important by the mid-nineteenth century, when the city was a centre for rail travel. Local ironfounders John Walker & Co, established around 1835, supplied the glorious ironwork for the British Museum railings around 1850, and found their niche in the provision of railings and gates to the surrounding estates. Confectionery was the sole industry to become established on a large scale in York; several firms were involved, of which Rowntrees was the largest, employing over 4,000 workers in 1909.

Lack of intrusive industry helped ensure that the medieval street plan survived relatively unscathed until the early nineteenth century. A brief bout of mid-Victorian road-widening did little to change the overall medieval-cum-Georgian appearance of the city, which York retains today.

Not only the medieval plan, but a significant number of medieval buildings remain. In the thirteenth century, York could boast over forty parish churches; this apparently large figure was not abnormal for a sizeable medieval city, but unusually, York has retained a substantial number of the original buildings. In the centre, nineteen medieval parish churches still stand, in whole or part, and all but St Olave's are within the walls. Current uses of these churches vary from arts and heritage centres through redundancy to fully-functioning places of worship.

The other great survivors from York's medieval heyday are the city walls, although, like the parish churches, they have undergone much repair and rebuilding. The original Roman wall, an earth bank topped by timber palisades, enclosed a rectangular area centred roughly on the site now occupied by the Minster; the palisades were replaced by a stone wall in the early second century. The present walls, which incorporate a small part of the Roman wall, follow the line of defences erected in Norman times; the process of adding stone walls to these defences lasted from the mid-thirteenth to the mid-fifteenth century. The city was then secured against attack by a combination of the walls, the castle and a lake to the east, the Fishpond of the Foss, which rendered a wall unnecessary. The fishpond resulted from the damming of the River Foss by William I, an initiative which brought water to the castle ditches and a supply of fish to its inhabitants.

Even before the walls were complete they were under repair, and their rebuilding and restoration has continued to this day. Repairs were necessary after the summer of 1644, when Parliamentarian troops successfully besieged the city, but the walls became redundant as functioning defences during the eighteenth century. The walls, and particularly the bars (or gateways), then became an obstacle to movement in and out of York, and the survival of the whole edifice was in doubt at the start of the nineteenth century; indeed, a short section south of Bootham Bar was lost at that time. However, restoration has since triumphed, and the walls have been a public walk since the end of the nineteenth century.

Although the concept of a walled city is romantic, the walls and bars are intrinsically fascinating, and walking the walls is an essential part of a visit to York, it cannot be said that the experience is sublime. Picturesque views of the Minster do not completely compensate for the townscape of busy roads, industrial developments, backyards and

Looking down on York from the Minster's central tower, 180 feet above the city roofscape.

York Minster from the south. The roof of the south transept was destroyed by fire on the 9th July 1984, but restoration has provided a fine new structure, complete with some unusual roof bosses (decorative elements covering the intersection of vaults).

offices. Often visitors walk only the walls neighbouring the Minster (making for many a close contact in the crowded summer season), but a ramble along the full two and three-quarter miles is worth the effort, to gain a feeling for the lay-out of the city, the close-packed nature of its centre, and the variety of its buildings.

As befits a defensive structure, for much of its length the wall presents an inaccessible face to the outer city (and a sheer drop on its inner side), so prospective walkers must make a start at either a bar or a tower, where steps lead to the stone-slabbed walkway.

Fishergate Tower, almost on the bank of the Foss at Fishergate, makes a good

The outer face of Walmgate Bar, the most easterly gateway through the city walls of York.

beginning. The tower dates from 1502 and its quaint tiled roof from 1740; Fishergate Bar, next on the anticlockwise route, was the original gateway in this area, but was burned in 1489 and closed. On the inner side of Walmgate Bar is an unusual structure, a timber-framed upper room, supported on stone Tuscan columns; it was probably an addition to the bar's domestic accommodation in the sixteenth century.

The Red Tower, dating from around 1490 but much reconstructed, marks the end of this length of wall, which reached the south bank of the Fishpond of the Foss. The walker now takes to Foss Islands Road, on the riverbank — the tall chimney on the right was built in 1900 for the city power station — and rejoins the wall across the traffic lights at Jewbury.

The church of St Cuthbert, just to the west, is one of the nineteen surviving medieval parish churches in the centre of the city. It was built largely in the fifteenth century, although elements of its eleventh-century predecessor appear in the east end. Just before the impressively tall Monk Bar, its superstructure a fourteenth century addition to the defences, watch for an ice-house dug into the outer base of the wall. Its domed, red-brick top is clearly visible; inside, the roughly egg-shaped space is about twenty feet high.

The next stage of the wall walk is a delight, with beautiful gardens and an idyllic view of the Minster. At Bootham Bar, the line of the wall continued south-west, but is now accessible only through the Yorkshire Museum gardens, so bear left along St Leonard's Place, passing the Theatre Royal. Its façade, a combination of gloomy Gothic bronze-yellow stone (1877-9) and elongated concrete mushrooms (1967-8) is remarkably uninspiring, but inside is a magnificent Art Nouveau auditorium, designed in 1901-2 by Frank Tugwell of Scarborough. A theatre was first built on the site in 1744, and many reconstructions have taken place; Tugwell is best known for his work on London's Savoy Theatre in 1929.

The red-brick dome of the ice house, adjoining the city wall near Monk Bar. Ice was stored in its roughly egg-shaped interior, which lies partly below ground level.

Turn right into Museum Street, and right again into the gardens; the Multangular Tower is ahead. It was the south-western corner of the Roman wall, and still rises to seventeen feet; its full height may have been around sixty feet. Inside the tower there are distinctive bands of red tiles, and the wall to the north is paralleled by structures of later date, including a Saxon tower; nowhere else in the city can the development of the wall be so clearly seen.

Leave the gardens to cross the Ouse at Lendal Tower where, between 1677 and 1846, water was taken from the river to supply the citizens of York, and distributed via a network of wooden pipes.

South of Lendal Bridge, which opened in 1863, the wall passes the huge North Eastern Railway headquarters offices. This massive construction, Edwardian Baroque on an enormous scale, was designed in 1900-6 by Horace Field and William Bell, and won a medal at the Paris Exhibition of 1905. There is some surprisingly delicate detailing for such a giant of a building, and the overall effect is not too overblown. Close to the offices, and almost beside the wall itself, stands the North Eastern Railway war memorial, an elegant obelisk and stone screen designed in 1922-4 by Sir Edwin Lutyens.

After the station the wall turns east, runs past colourful Micklegate Bar, and ends at the Old Baile on Cromwell Road, the site of one of York's original pair of castles. Cross Skeldergate Bridge and continue, bearing right, to Fishergate Tower and so complete the full circuit, but look for an elegant red-brick warehouse — now a restaurant — on the west bank of the Ouse, beside the bridge.

This is the York City Bond, built in 1872-3 by the city surveyor, George Styan. The bonded store, where goods could be kept until duties were paid, was erected in an unsuccessful attempt to improve the city's declining shipping trade.

Now for the city within the walls. Clifford's Tower, a good vantage point, is but a short stroll along Tower Street from Fishergate Tower. The mound upon which Clifford's Tower stands was the site of one of the two castles built by William I in 1068 and 1069. Both mounds were topped by wooden towers. The castle keep, known as Clifford's Tower since 1596, was built between 1245 and around 1272, and its plan, consisting of four connected semi-circular towers, was unique in England at that time. The geometric purity of the almost white, curving stone walls, and the hump of the green mound below, make this a most unusual monument, and a memorable starting point for a tour of the city.

Before setting out, look south to the open quadrangle of monumental eighteenth century buildings facing Clifford's Tower. On the far side is the Debtors' Prison, built in 1701-5 and probably designed by gentleman-architect William Wakefield of Huby Hall, about ten miles north of York. Wakefield's style was strongly influenced by Vanbrugh, and the massive nature of the Debtors' Prison — a clock tower and cupola top a central three-bay block which separates two wings — suggest Wakefield's hand, although he generally designed country houses. Clifford's Tower previously held some of the county's prisoners, but the Debtors' Prison, which housed offenders of all classes, provided greater security and comfort, with airy living quarters and a spacious exercise yard; it was thought by travellers to be one of the finest jails in Europe. The square is completed by a pair of almost identical, pedimented Classical buildings: to the west are the Assize Courts (1773-7), and opposite is the Female Prison (1780-3), both designed by John Carr.

Set out northward from Clifford's Tower along Castlegate, passing the elegant façade of another John Carr composition, Fairfax House, almost immediately on the right. It was expensively rebuilt for Viscount Fairfax of Emley from the early 1750s, although the excellent decorative plasterwork of the interior was not completed until 1762 or later. This town house is a fine example of the rebuilding which occurred in York around 1700-60, when timber-framed houses with overhanging upper stories were gradually replaced by substantial brick houses with polite architectural pretensions.

John Carr, a stonemason's son and self-taught architect, was born near Wakefield in 1723 and set up in practice in York during the 1750s. For the next forty years he designed country houses and public buildings throughout the North of England. His popularity with the gentry of Yorkshire resulted from his qualities as a practical architect; he was not an innovator, but his buildings always exhibited great craftsmanship, and eventually his work became widely respected.

Carr built several town houses in York, including Castlegate House (1763-5) almost opposite Fairfax House, and his own house by the Ouse in Skeldergate (1765-9, now demolished), and was twice lord mayor of the city. After his retirement, the practice was carried on by his assistant, Peter Atkinson; then followed Atkinson's son Peter, and grandsons John Bownas and William Atkinson. J B and W Atkinson did more work in mid-nineteenth century York than any other architectural practice.

The octagonal spire of St Mary, the tallest in York, beckons the walker along Castlegate. A sizeable church stood on the site in the eleventh century, but the present structure dates mainly from the fifteenth century, and was restored by William Butterfield in 1870.

Turn left down Friargate and right into Clifford Street, where the bumptious Romanesque façade of the Institute of Art, Science and Literature awaits.

It was built in 1883-5 by Walter Green Penty; the Penty architectural practice was another long-lived local firm. When Penty senior died in 1902, his son Frederick took over, while another son, A J Penty, left for London to pursue the architectural and social ideals of the Arts and Crafts Movement. In his Clifford Street building, W G Penty was perhaps inspired by the terracotta detailing of London's Natural History Museum. The institute, originally the Mechanics' Institute, later became a technical college and now houses, rather aptly, entertainment on the *Dracula* theme.

The neo-Baroque towers rising dramatically to the left top the façade of the law courts, a competition-winning design built in 1890-2 by Liverpool architect Huon Matear. A left along Cumberland Street takes you past the easily-missed façade of the Grand Opera House, constructed by theatre architect J P Briggs (once Frank Matcham's clerk of works) in 1902 from the carcase of a corn exchange and warehouse, which externally it still resembles. The auditorium, though, is perfectly theatrical, with a saucer-domed, sunburst ceiling.

Now down to the quayside and right along King's Staith, where there is a fine view of the mid-Victorian warehouses across the river on Queen's Staith, built in 1810-15 and initially used for landing coal. Climb the steps to the

Terracotta columns in the doorway of the Institute of Art, Science and Literature, built in 1883-5 by local architect Walter G Penty.

Ouse Bridge, where a diversion over the river is a possibility.

To explore west of the Ouse, follow Micklegate—a pleasantly curving street with some fine Georgian building—after crossing the bridge. In Trinity Lane, on the left, is Jacob's Well, a timber-framed house with an unnaturally large and well-carved door canopy, which probably dates from the late fifteenth century but originally belonged to a house over the river in Pavement.

The church of St Mary, Bishophill Junior, lies at the far end of Trinity Lane. Its tower, unspectacular but significant, is the oldest

The unusual wooden door-canopy of the timber-framed house known as Jacob's Well, situated in Trinity Lane. The carved canopy originally belonged to a house across the river on Pavement.

example of ecclesiastical architecture in the city, with re-used Roman stone at the base and Saxon bell-openings at the top. Return to Micklegate via St Martins Lane, passing the church of St Martin-cum-Gregory with its brick tower of 1844, and thence back over the Ouse Bridge.

At the bridge, head east along Low Ousegate, passing St Michael Spurriergate on the left; this church was converted to parish offices, combined with other secular uses, in 1989. Its Perpendicular exterior hides a beautiful interior, restored in 1965, strong in eighteenth century elements and with some fine stained glass, including an early fifteenth century Jesse window (one which shows the genealogy of Christ's descent).

Straight on into High Ousegate, and the distinctive octagonal, openwork tower of All Saints Church, Pavement rises above the busy junction at its far end. Here there is a delightful, thirteenth century, door-closing ring in the shape of a beast's head, and late fourteenth century stained glass in the west window. Glass from just before this period is unusual in York, as the glass-painters suffered during repeated visits from the Black Death in the mid-fourteenth century. The elegant tower was built in 1475-1501.

Opposite the church, on the corner of High Ousegate and Parliament Street, is the striking red façade of Barclays Bank, its Gothic style and harsh materials thought utterly tasteless for many years. The bank was erected in 1901 by Liverpool architect Edmund Kirby, and it cannot be said to have weathered or mellowed in the least over the past century or so. The terracotta façade is a fine example of decorative ceramics and looks as fresh as the

A detail of the elaborate carving on the door-canopy at Jacob's Well, Trinity Lane.

day it was built; it is a wonderfully colourful contrast to an occasionally bland cityscape.

Turn right past All Saints into Piccadilly, and the timber-framed Merchant Adventurers' Hall is soon visible to the left. It was built in 1357-61 for a religious guild whose membership was strong in textile merchants or mercers. This influential body was effectively the mercers' trade guild, and was more powerful than the local craft guilds. It became a merchants' company in 1430 and, with the granting of a royal charter in 1581, the Company of Merchant Adventurers. Their main concern was the expanding export trade in woollens. The undercroft or lower part of the Merchant Adventurers' Hall was used as a hospital, taking in selected almspeople, and its walls contain the oldest bricks in the city. A row of mighty oak posts runs down the centre of the undercroft, supporting the great

The brick-built tower of medieval St Margaret's Church, off Walmgate. The seventeenth century tower replaced an earlier version, which collapsed.

hall above, which has superlative timber-frame construction.

A short cut through the grounds of the Merchant Adventurers' Hall leads into Fossgate, but a diversion across the Foss will take the walker past one of the great sights of Victorian York. Follow Piccadilly over the Foss, then bear left into Merchantgate and right along Walmgate. To the right in St Denys Road is the much-altered church of St Denys, with a Norman south doorway and the only thirteenth century stained glass to be found in any of the city's parish churches. There is also a unique reredos (until recently, hidden under flock wallpaper) of splendidly colourful nineteenth century hand-painted tiles.

Leave Walmgate by Paver Lane, bearing right at the corner into Percy's Lane, and meet Navigation Road at St Margaret's Church, largely rebuilt in 1851-2, although a church has occupied this site since the twelfth century. The brick tower was erected in 1684-5 to replace a previous west tower which collapsed. The fine Norman doorway, showing the signs of the zodiac and assorted strange beasts, originated at St Nicholas' Hospital.

Behind the metal grille is the Norman doorway of St Margaret's The stone carvings include mythological beasts and the signs of the zodiac.

DO IN REMEMBRANCE O

Inside the Church of St Denys, on St Denys Road, is this reredos of nineteenth century hand-painted tiles. It is possible that the tiles were painted by local stained-glass artists.

This was the largest of the city's four leper hospitals sited outside the walls; St Nicholas was in existence by the early twelfth century, and was ruined during the 1644 siege of York.

Turn left along Navigation Road. At its end is the River Foss and, heading left, a path which leads on to a slightly unnerving metal walkway, running alongside the mammoth red-brick Leethams Warehouse and across the river to Rowntree's Wharf.

The twenty-two bay warehouse was built in 1895-6 by W G Penty for the York-based firm of Leethams; it served a nearby flour mill, which was burnt down in 1931. The huge structure, now converted for business and residential use, commands the junction between the canalised Foss and Wormald's Cut. The warehouse rears up over the waters to an embattled peak, with a turret reaching nine stories in height; it is a landmark

The Church of St Denys has been much altered, but there is some excellent stained glass to be seen in the unusual interior.

The massive Ionic portico of the Central Methodist Church in St Saviourgate. The church was built for the Wesleyans in 1839-40.

Merchant Adventurers' Hall. Head right, past the monumental Baroque archway of Macdonalds furniture shop. The showy, buff ceramic façade originally belonged to the Electric Cinema, the first purpose-built cinema in York, opened by National Electric Theatres of London in 1911. The architect was local man William Whincup, who produced a fashionable façade in cream and white Doulton ware; the cinema became a shop in 1957. Continue along and cross the road to pass the Blue Bell, a tiny pub with two happily timeless bars.

At the end of Fossgate, take the second right into St Saviourgate; the impressive portico on the left, displaying a set of giant Ionic columns, belongs to the Centenary Chapel (now Central Methodist Church) built in 1839-40 by James Simpson of Leeds, a specialist in methodist chapels, for the Wesleyans.

The church of St Saviour, currently doing duty as an archaeology centre, is further down the elegant, mainly Georgian street of St Saviourgate. There was a church on the site in the eleventh century, and the tower is fifteenth century, but the present appearance of the church — a self-effacing Gothic pile — dates from a reconstruction of the aisles in 1844-5 by Richard Hey Sharp. Sharp was first pupil then partner of Peter Atkinson junior, setting up on his own account at 18 St Saviourgate in 1827.

Left, right and left again will bring the walker to Aldwark and the Merchant Taylors' Hall, an outwardly inconspicuous brick building which encloses a surprising timber-framed interior, the only surviving meeting-place of a local craft guild. The hall dates from

throughout York, but can only be properly appreciated in the intimate confines of walkway, wharf and water.

Slip through the gap in the wall at the far end of the wharf, bearing left along an alley to emerge on Fossgate, almost opposite the

The elegant Georgian doorcase of 24, St Saviourgate. The substantial, three-bay house was built around 1763.

around 1400, although the external brick walls were probably an eighteenth century improvement. Internally, the timber roof-structure was also hidden by a later plaster ceiling, but recent restoration has revealed the original in all its glory; a tribute to changing tastes.

Bear left into Goodramgate then right into College Street, dominated by the magnificent east window of the Minster. Opposite, and on a rather smaller scale, is St William's College,

built from about 1465 to accommodate a community of chantry priests (those endowed to sing masses) from the Minster.

The delightful central quadrangle and multiplicity of doorways suggests a collegiate design, with several stairs giving access to small rooms. St William's College was dissolved in 1546, and the premises have since been used as a private house, shops and meeting rooms; fortunately, the inevitable changes in plan have not obscured the

Reflections of Leethams Warehouse in the waters of the River Foss. The massive warehouse was built in 1895-6, and has now been converted for residential and business use.

The massive form of Leethams Warehouse, built in 1895-6 by Walter G Penty, overlooks the junction between the canalised River Foss (left) and Wormald's Cut.

fifteenth century carpentry or detracted from the atmospheric quality of this rare medieval survivor.

To stroll around the outside of the Minster, continue along Minster Yard and then bear left past the chapter house into Dean's Park; the Minster may be entered at its west end.

First, though, look out for the prominent pair of twin gables on the stone façade of the Treasurer's House to the right; this was originally the home of the Treasurer of the Minster — a richly-rewarded office — and was built in the late eleventh century, although the present structure is mainly sixteenth to eighteenth century work. The last treasurer resigned in 1547, after which the house saw a rapid succession of owners, including John Aislabie, creator of the magnificent Studley Royal landscape garden near Ripon, in the late seventeenth century. The house was extensively restored in 1897, which is probably when the kitchen was lined with blue and white Dutch tiles dating from the late nineteenth century. They portray a wide variety of landscapes and children's games, including skipping and leap-frog.

Dean's Park is always a peaceful contrast to the bustling city; the ruined Norman arcade of the Archbishop's Palace sits amidst the greenery, while the octagonal geometry

A detail from the Baroque, ceramic façade of York's first purpose-built cinema, the Electric (now Macdonalds furniture shop), on Fossgate. It dates from 1911.

Flying buttresses above the south aisle of the Minster nave, looking towards the west front. Although medieval in appearance, the flying buttresses were added in 1905-7 by G F Bodley.

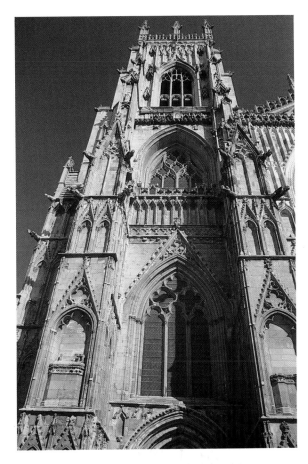

The west front of York Minster, built during the late thirteenth and early fourteenth centuries. The great west window portrays the 'Heart of Yorkshire' and dates from 1338.

The Boer War memorial on High Petergate, designed by G F Bodley in 1905. A total of 1,320 Yorkshiremen died in the war.

of the chapter house is best appreciated, at least initially, from the outside.

York Minster, the Cathedral of St Peter, originated with a small wooden church founded near the present site in AD 627 by Edwin, King of Northumbria. This structure was soon replaced by a stone church, which was burnt down in 1069; rebuilding took place around 1080, and after another fire in 1137, the great Gothic cathedral itself was begun by Archbishop Gray in 1220. The material was limestone from Tadcaster, and building work was not completed until 1472.

The story of the construction of the Minster is complex — the central tower collapsed in 1407 during a storm — but the end result is a particularly high-quality display of the evolution of Gothic style in England. The nave was built between 1291 and the 1350s in the Decorated style, the chancel followed in the latter part of the fourteenth century, while the central tower (which gives a wonderful view over the city) is early fifteenth century. The late thirteenth century chapter house is one of only two such polygonal structures in Britain without a central support; its roof, which reaches over sixty-six feet in height, is an intricate wooden vault. The floor, of decorative Minton tiles, dates from restoration in 1844-5.

Although the Minster gives every impression of strength and solidity, in the 1960s it became apparent that the foundations of the 180 foot central tower were slowly giving way beneath the weight of masonry, which produced a load of 4,000 tons on each of the four main pillars. Underpinning the tower with concrete took six years and was completed in 1972, creating a new undercroft. Fire, probably caused by an electrical storm, destroyed the roof of the south transept in the early morning of the 9th July 1984, but restoration work, which included the rose window, made good the damage in only a few years.

The fine array of stained glass in the Minster dates mainly from the fourteenth and fifteenth centuries, although there is a significant amount from the twelfth century. The magnificent east window, the largest single area of medieval stained glass in the world, was commissioned from the glazier John Thornton of Coventry in 1405. It took three years to construct and shows a Christian view of world history, beginning with genesis and ending with the revelation. A portrait of the window's donor, Walter Skirlaw, Bishop of Durham, occupies the centre of the bottom row of panels. Another highlight of the Minster's glass may be found in the Zouche Chapel, off the south aisle of the chancel. Here, delicate birds and monkeys play on tiny, diamond-shaped panes in the south windows; they date from the fifteenth century.

It would be easy, and enjoyable, to spend all day in the Minster, unravelling the stories told in stained glass, climbing the tower and exploring the undercroft, but there is still more to see of the city.

From the west end of the Minster, head left along High Petergate, passing the delicate neo-Gothic Boer War memorial designed in 1905 by G F Bodley. The octagonal column commemorates the 1,320 Yorkshiremen who died in the war. To the left is St Michael-le-Belfrey, where Guy Fawkes was baptised in 1570. The church was completely rebuilt in 1525-37 by the Minster's master-mason, John Forman, although the openwork turret and the squat west front are mid-Victorian.

Turn right into Stonegate (look back for a fine Minster view), a medieval street with houses dating from the fourteenth to nineteenth centuries, and some intriguing

A cheerful collection of modern gargoyles adorns a pinnacle above the south aisle of the nave at York Minster.

Fifteen English kings on the pulpitum, or chancel screen, look down on the new foundations of York Minster in June 1971.

Left: *Underpinning the central tower of York Minster in 1971; the concrete foundations seen from above.*

Part of the west front of York Minster, which overlooks the mainly Georgian street of High Petergate.

shopfronts. Especially peculiar is number ten, towards the south end on the right; here the builder used Victorian encaustic tiles, made by Maw & Co and normally to be found on floors, to face the upper part of the shop. The result is surprisingly decorative and effective. The end of Stonegate is marked by St Helen's Church, with its fifteenth century octagonal lantern; it was the parish church of the York glass-painters.

A glance to the right along Blake Street will take in the splendid portico of the Assembly Rooms, designed by the renowned gentleman-architect Richard Boyle, third Earl of Burlington, in 1731-2. Burlington, whose country home was at Londesborough, fifteen miles east of York, was a pioneer in the use of the Palladian style, and the main hall of the Assembly Rooms is an exact copy of Palladio's Egyptian Hall. The airy hall, over 100 feet long, is lined by Corinthian columns which support an elegant clerestory.

The success of the Assembly Rooms, which housed concerts, balls and the like, confirmed the importance of York as a social centre — indeed, the social capital of Yorkshire — in the early eighteenth century. The Ionic portico, which forms a suitably impressive façade, is actually an addition of 1828; it was the work of local architect James Pigott Pritchett, then in partnership with Charles and William Watson. Pritchett, an ecclesiastical specialist with a good grasp of the technicalities of building, practised throughout Yorkshire, and produced three sons who also became architects.

Across St Helens Square is the steadfast façade of the Mansion House, built in 1726-33 as the official residence of the lord mayor. Behind the Ionic pilasters, the two upper floors

The fifteenth-century lantern of much-restored St Helen's Church. This prominent landmark stands opposite the Mansion House on St Helens Square.

form one great chamber, the state room. Turn left into Coney Street, where a great clock-face hangs above the throng. It is suspended from the east wall of St Martin-le-Grand, a fifteenth century church which was almost destroyed by an air raid in 1942; restoration in 1961-8 by George G Pace contrived to produce a church from the remains. The clock itself dates from 1668.

Just opposite the church, take New Street, then turn right into Davygate, which leads to St Sampsons Square. The Three Cranes public house, which faces the square, has a delightful ceramic panel of the eponymous birds above its entrance; the panel probably dates from the 1930s.

Before heading along Church Street, on the far side of the pub, look down Feasegate (at the opposite end of the square), to see an unusual shopfront on the right at numbers five to seven; it dates from 1885. This was a radical design for its time, with slim, cast iron columns dividing huge areas of glazing. The iron was produced by local ironfounders Thomlinson-Walker, originally John Walker & Co.

Underneath Church Street lies a 150 foot length of Roman sewer, a fine structure, and as sturdy as any Roman fortification. The main branch is four feet high and two to three feet wide, and is built of of large sandstone and millstone grit blocks.

Pass St Sampson's, a medieval church rebuilt in 1848, and turn right into Patrick Pool; this leads into Little Shambles, where a passage left will take the walker into the Shambles, a narrow, picturesque street of overhanging, timber-framed houses. The later medieval ground plan was often long and narrow, with the house, only a single room in width, sited at right angles to the street. The overhang was not a structural necessity, but was a matter of show — merely a fashion of the day.

Walk left along the Shambles, along Kings Court, and bear right into Goodramgate. Look for a gateway on the left, just before a terrace of timber-framed houses known as Lady Row; these are some of the oldest houses in York, and were built around 1316. Go through the gate into the beautifully-secluded churchyard of Holy Trinity, a parish church which has one of the most memorable interiors in the whole of the city.

Holy Trinity has a complex building history, covering the twelfth to fifteenth centuries, and excellent fifteenth century stained glass in the east window. It was donated by the rector, John Walker, in 1471; some of the figures portrayed relate to local guilds, in which Walker played an important role.

The true delight of Holy Trinity is the assembly of box pews arranged in unlikely attitudes on a stone slab floor which rises and falls as it pleases. No right angles here. Most of the furniture, including the two-decker pulpit, is eighteenth century, and luckily escaped Victorian renewal. The church, now redundant, is perfect for peaceful contemplation, not only of oaken pews staggering down the nave, but of the wealth of the city's architecture, stretching back around 1,700 years, from the glory of the Minster's renewed south transept to the efficiency of the Roman sewer system.

YORK WITHOUT

The Buildings of Outer York

S PEND TOO long within the walls of York and a surfeit of medievalism might result. The cure is an exploration of the city without, where Georgian domesticity and Victorian technology intermingle with contributions from medieval and modern times, enticing the traveller into lesser-known York.

Begin at the westernmost gateway, Micklegate Bar, and cross into Blossom Street, where the stern Georgian façade of the Bar Convent overlooks the junction.

The convent was opened in 1686 for the education of Catholic girls, and the present building was designed by Thomas Atkinson — not a member of the local architectural dynasty, but a Yorkshireman and a Catholic — between 1766 and 1786. The excellent Classical chapel, with its hint of Baroque, dates from 1766-9 and is the highlight of the original interior. More immediately attractive is the sleek and colourful expanse of nineteenth-century encaustic tiles which form the floor of a newly-created conservatory; the modern glazed roof is elegant and thoroughly in keeping.

Head down Blossom Street, passing a fine example of a 1930s car showroom (currently disused) on the far side, to the Odeon, a typically stylish Harry Weedon design of 1937, all strong verticals and broad curves. Unusually, it was carried out in brick rather than the normal glazed ceramics, as a concession to the historic surroundings, but — fortunately — such is the power of the façade that the impact is barely reduced. In a quarter mile, past the Georgian houses of the Mount, Elm Bank (now an hotel) stands on the corner of Love Lane. It was the house of Sidney Leetham, the miller whose warehouse was built by W G Penty near Navigation Road in 1895-6.

Elm Bank was put up around 1870, but its present interior, one of the most exciting in the city, was created about 1898 by the combined talents of Penty's son Arthur and George Walton, a fashionable designer from Glasgow. Walton — a contemporary of Charles

Rennie Mackintosh — expanded his business to London in 1897 and to York, with a shop in Stonegate, the following year. Walton was responsible for even the tiniest details of his interiors, and normally used an idiosyncratic combination of Art Nouveau, Arts and Crafts, and gently Classical stylistic elements. Elm Bank veers towards the Art Nouveau, with masses of colour in the stained glass and the wall paintings, the latter set with glass jewels.

A little further down the Tadcaster road on the right is St George's Place, where Bishopsbarns, the home of architect Walter Henry Brierley, may be found. In 1885 Brierley began to work with James Demaine, who had taken over the architectural practice begun by John Carr and carried on by the Atkinsons. Brierley eventually became a sole practitioner, building widely throughout Yorkshire in a neo-Renaissance style, as well as being architect to the North Riding County Council and

The unusual brick-built Odeon cinema on Blossom Street, designed by Harry Weedon, was one of thirty-six Odeons erected in 1937.

the Diocese of York. His own house, which dates from 1905, is a homely English classic, which makes good use of traditional materials. A mile further down the Tadcaster road at Dringhouses is another Brierley house, Goddards; this rambling, brick-built Tudor mansion, erected in 1926-7, was one of the architect's last works.

To explore the outskirts east of the Ouse, head back into the city and over the river at Skeldergate Bridge. Turn south again, along Fishergate; any of the narrow streets which soon lead off to the right will take you to the riverbank and New Walk, a tree-lined promenade begun in 1733. Fashionable terraces sprouted at right angles to the walk over the next century or so, one of the best being New Walk Terrace, with a combination of elegant Regency and heftier Victorian houses.

Return to Fishergate and look for Cemetery Road on the left, which leads back towards the city centre. The entrance to one of the city's most impressive and least-known architectural sites, deeply evocative of the Victorian era, is marked by a stolid Greek Revival gatehouse (now minus its Ionic portico); this is York Cemetery, opened in 1837 by the York Public Cemetery Company.

Burial arrangements for the citizens of York had previously comprised the medieval parish churchyards, augmented by a few Nonconformist burial grounds. The difficulty of finding space for the bodies of the 185 people killed in the cholera outbreak of 1832 led to agitation for a new cemetery, and in 1834 subscriptions were invited for its establishment by a committee, which became the cemetery company in 1836.

The portico of the chapel at York Cemetery, designed by James Pigott Pritchett senior in 1837. The chapel deteriorated to such an extent that the roof collapsed in 1984, but restoration has been in progress since 1987.

York Cemetery, opened in 1837 by the York Public Cemetery Company, and now a haven for wildlife.

The company's architect was James Pigott Pritchett senior, who provided a plan which included a chapel, walls and a gate lodge; the elegant lay-out of paths, combining a cross, two circles and gentle curves, also seems to have been by his hand. The design of the white stone, Greek Revival-style chapel was based on the temple of Erectheus in Athens. It was consecrated on the 15th September 1837,

although the first burial in the Church of England section of the cemetery (there was also a Dissenters area) did not take place until the following month.

To explore the cemetery, go through the cast iron gates, which date from 1880. They replaced the original gates, which were manufactured by the iron foundry of John Walker & Co in Walmgate. Follow any of the

A row of gravestones amidst the luxuriant vegetation of York Cemetery.

circuitous paths which wind between the gravestones, some almost hidden amongst the trees, flowers and brambles. Luxuriant planting made the cemetery into one of York's most interesting walks, freely open to the public except on Sundays, but the company was troubled by those visitors who picked flowers or even stole plants.

One of the most eye-catching monuments in the cemetery is the frilly Gothic canopy which stands a little to the east of the chapel. It is a memorial to lawyer and alderman Jonathan Gray, first chairman of the cemetery company; below is the family vault. The memorial, also designed by Pritchett, dates from 1837, so it seems the architect — or more probably the client — was happy to combine Gothic and Greek Revival themes. Certainly the lavish stonework fits in perfectly with the picturesque lay-out, which holds memorials to several of the major York families.

The cemetery was reasonably successful in its early years, although charges were high, and its area was eventually extended several times. But during the twentieth century, as the available space for burials diminished and costs of maintenance increased, the cemetery company lost enthusiasm for the undertaking. The company went into liquidation in 1966, and the cemetery gradually became more neglected; liquidators ensured that all possible assets were sold, including the woodwork and panelling of the chapel.

However, in the 1980s the real worth of the site and buildings became apparent to the city, when fashions in funerary monuments and Victorian architecture changed, and since 1988 the cemetery has been in the care of the York Cemetery Trust, who are restoring buildings and managing the planting. Like a rambling but quiet and secluded garden, York Cemetery makes a delightful contrast to the packed streets of the medieval city.

Turn right from the cemetery gates to pass alongside the boundary wall, which is capped by an intimidating sarcophagus at its northwest corner. Next-but-one on the right is Heslington Road, which in a mile, via University Road, leads to the campus of the University of York.

The first attempt to found a university at York was made in 1641, but it took until 1960 before the university was established, and a further five years before the initial buildings were opened. The campus is located in the 185-acre grounds of Heslington Hall, a brick-built mansion erected in 1565-8 but much altered in 1852-5 and 1876, while the interior is mainly by Brierley and dates from 1903.

The modern buildings of the university run west from the hall, and are centred on an artificial lake which provides a superb focus for the generally anonymous collection of laboratories, halls of residence and the like which nestle amongst the planting. Their appearance results from the adoption of CLASP, a system of prefabricated components often used for school buildings; cladding panels cover steel frames. The single outstanding feature is the water tower, a huge concrete mushroom erupting beside the chemistry laboratories to the north of the site. University architects Robert Matthew, Johnson-Marshall and Partners were forced to add the tower at a late stage in site planning. But for its obvious utility, the tower has some of the qualities of a good folly: fortuitous, symbolic and eye-catching.

If a detour to the university is too time-consuming, turn left after about a quarter mile of Heslington Road into Wellington Street, then take narrow Lawrence Lane. On the left is the lofty and overbearing church of St Lawrence, built in 1883-92 by J G Hall of Canterbury, using the Early English style.

Rather more interesting is the adjoining tower of Old St Lawrence, all which now remains of the medieval church where the architect Sir John Vanbrugh was married on the 14th January 1719. It was demolished in 1881-3. The tower is thirteenth century, although the pretty, pierced parapet dates from the fifteenth; the Norman doorway (complete with monster), was originally part of the Old Hospital Chapel of St Nicholas, demolished in the nineteenth century.

The old tower (foreground) and the new Church of St Lawrence. Apart from its tower, the original church was demolished between 1881 and 1883, when work began on building its replacement.

The Gray family memorial in York Cemetery. Jonathan Gray was the first chairman of York Public Cemetery Company, which opened the cemetery in 1837.

The massive sarcophagus of painter William Etty lies in St Olave's churchyard, York, close to the ruins of St Mary's Abbey. Beyond, in the distance, is the Greek Revival façade of the Yorkshire Museum. Etty died in 1849.

Turn left into Lawrence Street and head back towards Walmgate Bar; on the left, in Paragon Street, is the new Barbican Centre, an arts and sports centre in pale buff blockwork. The skyline saves the building

from dullness, but sadly it is afflicted with that disease common in late twentieth century architecture: lack of an obvious entrance. It is possible to pass an entertaining few moments in the coffee bar, watching the attempts of those outside to crack the entry code, heaving and pushing at unyielding sections of glazed wall.

At the bar, turn north along Foss Islands Road, soon passing close to an impressively tall chimney, now standing alone, but once part of the corporation's electricity generating station which opened in February 1900. The brick decoration at its tip is particularly elegant. Power was generated by burning coal, supplemented by heat from the rubbish incinerator at the adjacent corporation refuse works. The generating station provided light for streets, public buildings and homes; the 4,630 lamps lit by the station in April 1900 had almost quadrupled within a year, and several extensions were made to the generating plant to cope with demand in the early years.

Foss Islands road meets Layerthorpe at a busy, staggered crossing; head straight over and into Foss Bank, where a shapely and decorative Victorian cast iron gasholder rears up on the right. The gas works dates from 1880-5, and was an extension of the York United Gas Light Company's works on the west bank of the Foss. Late Victorian gasholders were not always strictly functional in design, and this specimen is an excellent example of openwork cast iron, making the entire structure appear lightweight and surprisingly delicate.

To return to Georgian York, follow Foss Bank as it bends westward, then cross Monkgate into Grove Street, which continues for a quarter mile or so to Clarence Street. There, turn right, then first left into Hospital Lane, soon passing Bootham Park Hospital, built by John Carr in 1774-7 as the York Lunatic Asylum.

The asylum was established in 1772 to cater

The chimney of the old electricity generating station on Foss Islands Road. The stack dates from 1900 and is a well-known York landmark.

for the paupers of the city and county, but although sufficient monies were eventually subscribed to ensure construction was completed, nothing was left for the care of those too poor to pay for their upkeep, and wealthy patients were admitted from 1784 to provide a source of funds. A prolonged struggle to improve the administration of the hospital ensued, leading to administrative reforms in 1814. The eleven-bay, red-brick structure has a row of arched windows set in blank arches along the main floor, almost reminiscent of Carr's stable designs. Inside, fine Minton floor

This decorative Victorian cast iron gasholder, dating from 1880-5, rises above the gasworks beside Foss Bank.

tiles, a nineteenth century addition, line the lengthy corridors.

Once past the hospital, cross the Scarborough railway line by the footbridge and head left along Grosvenor Terrace to Bootham. Half a mile to the right is the village of Clifton, centred on triangular Clifton Green. Georgian and early Victorian expansion bridged the gap between the original village and the city, but the suburb still has a sense of identity, reinforced by the presence of church and pub. The latter, with a fine shell-hooded porch, was designed by W G Penty. The church dates from 1866-7, but perhaps more interesting is the red-brick Methodist church, imposing and steepled, which was built in 1909 by local architect Edward Taylor.

Returning towards Bootham Bar, look out for St Peter's School on the right. St Peter's was the original Minster school, dating from the seventh century; it was re-founded in 1557 but, after a downturn in its fortunes, left the Minster precinct to amalgamate with the Proprietary School Company at Clifton in 1844.

The company's new buildings, begun in 1838, were designed by John Harper in a glorious, ornate Gothic style, although many additions have since been made. York artist and architect Harper had recently been one of the unlucky contestants in the competition to design the new Houses of Parliament, after the 1834 fire; perhaps the Gothic turrets of St Peter's provided some consolation.

Glance left on the return to Bootham Bar, after passing Grosvenor Terrace, towards what used to be the grounds of Bootham Park Hospital. York's first Fine Art and Industrial Exhibition was held here between the 24th

The main pavilion of York's first Fine Art and Industrial Exhibition.

July and the 31st October 1866; a total of around 338,000 visitors entered the main pavilion, a temporary structure of timber and glass with a jolly Gothic façade, which was designed by Edward Taylor in consultation with J B and W Atkinson. The success of the exhibition, one of many following in the wake of the 1851 Great Exhibition, encouraged the organisers to attempt another, and a site was found a quarter mile distant along Bootham, in the grounds of St Mary's Abbey opposite Bootham Bar.

The new, permanent exhibition building (eventually to become the City Art Gallery) opened on the 7th May 1879. Edward Taylor was again the architect, and he produced a rather quiet, Renaissance design with a repeated arch motif in windows and arcades. The only showy elements in this distinctly non-exhibitionist building are the two colourful tile panels on the façade, depicting Leonardo and Michelangelo (although even these may be a later addition, perhaps from around 1887).

The exhibition itself, which closed in November 1879, went well, with around 530,000 visitors passing through the main building and a temporary wooden extension to the rear, to see works of art and an assortment of industrial items. Surprisingly, the temporary hall survived until 1941, and Taylor's main hall, now his best-known work in York, fulfils its original purpose as the City Art Gallery.

Just to the south of the art gallery is King's Manor, a fascinating building which began life as the abbot's house of St Mary's Abbey, and is now part of the University of York. The history of both manor and abbey may best be disentangled from the park to the rear of King's Manor, the Museum Gardens, so turn back into Bootham and take the first left, Marygate.

St Olave's Church, marking the gateway to the gardens, is an amalgam of original medieval work, eighteenth century rebuilding and a nineteenth century chancel interior. The church was damaged when used as a gun platform in the Civil War, necessitating the 1721-2 reconstruction. In the churchyard — an enclosed and silent domain which may be seen from the gardens — is a monumental sarcophagus dedicated to the painter William Etty, who died in 1849. Etty was the son of a local miller and confectioner with a shop in Feasegate. Unusually for an English artist, he specialised in paintings of nudes, and also campaigned for the conservation of York's old buildings.

There is much to ponder in the Museum Gardens. On the left are the ruins of St Mary's Abbey, a Benedictine foundation established just outside the city walls by William Rufus in 1089. The most impressive remaining stonework — an arcade of pointed windows, their tracery almost gone — formed the north aisle wall of the late thirteenth century church, which was a large and spectacular construction, 350 feet in length. After dissolution, and especially during the eighteenth century, most of the abbey's masonry was removed to supply local building projects. The abbey wall, which surrounded the twelve-acre precinct, has fared better — indeed better than any other example of English monastic walling. It was completed in the fourteenth century and may easily be seen on Marygate.

In 1827 the Yorkshire Philosophical Society was granted a lease of the abbey ruins with three acres of adjoining land, and immediately began to build a museum, the Greek Revival structure to the east of the ruins. Their chosen architect was William Wilkins, who insisted on Greek Revival style as he felt any contemporary Gothic building, although fashionable, would be overwhelmed by York's abundance of medieval architecture.

Wilkins, who went on to design the National Gallery in 1834-8, was a great scholar of Classical architecture and protagonist of the Greek Revival. His museum-as-temple, with its Greek Doric portico (albeit technically incorrect, as the spacing between the columns is uneven), was ideal for the newly-formed Philosophical Society, which needed a suitably imposing base for the promotion of its scientific ideas. The museum opened in 1830. The addition to the rear, an early example of reinforced concrete construction, dates from 1912; its façade is in matching Greek style. Would Wilkins have considered it theoretically unsound?

The ruins of St Mary's Abbey, seen from within St Olave's churchyard. This series of arches formed the north aisle wall of the late thirteenth century abbey church.

Behind the Yorkshire Museum is King's Manor. It was built as the abbot's house in the late thirteenth century, and rebuilt in brick between 1483 and the early sixteenth century. In fact it is more mansion than house, and after the Dissolution it became home to the President of the Council of the North, instituted by Richard III to administer Northern England.

The various presidents first changed the orientation of King's Manor, moving its main entrance from the abbey frontage to Bootham Bar, then altered and enlarged the accommodation. After the council was abolished in 1641,

Looking west from the crossing tower of the Minster, with St Mary's Abbey on the left in the middle distance.

the manor was used for dwelling houses, workshops, an assembly room and a series of schools, until it was bought by the corporation in 1958 and eventually became part of the university. The best architectural features of King's Manor — chimneypieces and rich plasterwork — date from the century of occupation by the Council of the North, but the entire building, a rambling and confusing collection of rooms, is a delightful architectural mixture, ranging in time across nearly 700 years.

In front of the museum, gardens run down to the Ouse, past the Philosophical Society's observatory, built in 1833, and the *hospitium* or guest-house of the abbey. This much-restored but picturesque structure, with its stone-built ground floor and timber-framed upper storey, is now part of the museum.

Leave the Museum Gardens by the eastern gate and turn right into Museum Street, crossing the Ouse on Lendal Bridge. Bear right under the city wall, through an arch cut to provide better access to the railway station, and head towards the yellow-brick bulk of the Royal Station Hotel. The station itself is just beyond. The *porte cochere* leads into the bustle of the trainshed; navigate across to the platform's edge for a first glimpse of the breathtaking curve of the arched iron and glass roof, a magnificent piece of railway architecture.

York's original railway station, a terminus, stood just east of the present station and inside the city walls, which were breached by two arches near their south-west extremity to allow the trains access. It was opened in 1841 by a combination of two companies, the York & North Midland Railway and the Great North of England Railway, whose lines, approaching from Leeds and Darlington respectively, met just outside the walls.

Prior to 1841 there was a temporary terminus in Queen Street. The architect chosen to design the new terminus was George Townsend Andrews of York, assisted by the engineers of the two companies involved, Thomas Cabrey for the York & North Midland and Thomas Storey for the Great North of England.

For this early station, Andrews produced an innovative U-shaped plan; it was the first terminus to have a continuous range of buildings enclosing the track on three sides, completed when the Station Hotel was added in 1853. As railway traffic through York increased, working the terminus became increasingly difficult, since through-trains had to reverse to leave the station. Passengers for the various railway lines mixed chaotically, and accidents were frequent. Although additional platforms were brought into use, the North Eastern Railway (formed on the 31st July 1854 by an amalgamation of the York & North Midland with two other companies) decided in 1865 to build a completely new station outside the restrictive city walls.

Much of the old station still exists, although very little of the trainshed remains. Its main front faces Tanner Row, round the corner from the mighty North Eastern Railway headquarters office building. It is still in use for railway administration, and serves as a monument to the co-operation between two York men who were of considerable importance to railway construction throughout north-east England, G T Andrews and George Hudson, chairman of the York & North

The end-screens at the south end of the trainshed of York railway station, built in 1872-7 for the North Eastern Railway.

Midland, who became known as the 'Railway King'.

Hudson, originally a draper, was mayor of York in 1839, and thus able to influence the city's attitude to the railways. He was deeply involved in the railway mania which peaked in 1846, by which time he controlled almost half of England's railways. Andrews became sheriff of York, and won many contracts for stations on Hudson's lines. Together they produced some fine railway architecture, but in 1855, the year of Andrews' death, Hudson went into exile away from Britain. His public face as a railway entrepreneur had been exposed as a front for a variety of fraudulent behaviour, which cost investors and other railway companies many thousands of pounds.

The construction of York's new railway station, in the post-Hudson era, was not without difficulties. Seven years elapsed between the decision to build and the start of construction in 1872, largely due to financial problems within the North Eastern Railway, and it was 1877 before the station was complete. The architects were the first three men to be employed by the North Eastern Railway as company architects: Thomas Prosser, who held the post in 1857-74, Benjamin Burleigh (1874-6) and William Peachey (1876-7). Prosser produced the original plan, which his successors carried out and modified.

Although the *porte cochere* makes a pleasant introduction to the station, it is rather less memorable than the spectacular trainshed. It is the most impressive in the country outside London; the length of the main platform is 1,500 feet, while the roof covers a maximum of 850 feet. Structurally, the trainshed comprises four roof spans supported by three rows of cast iron columns, nearly 100 in total, with brick side-walls. The columns carry wrought iron girders, with heraldic decoration; the roof ribs are also of wrought iron. Even the paraphernalia associated with electrification of the East Coast line has not reduced the impact of light falling from the curving shed roof.

Leave the station foyer, where a tile map of the North Eastern Railway network in the early twentieth century is displayed (the work of Craven Dunnill & Co of Jackfield in Shropshire), to stroll north along the platform. On the right is a delightful little domed pavilion in Art Nouveau style with fine, colourful stained glass, now in use as a model railway centre. This was originally the tea room, and

Under the clock in the curving trainshed at York railway station.

was designed by the company architect William Bell in 1906.

Heading out of the station, past the tea room, the octagonal lobby of the Royal Station Hotel appears to the left, paved with encaustic floor tiles in a radial pattern. The yellow-brick hotel, designed in a vaguely Italianate style by William Peachey, was built in 1877-8 and extended in 1882 and 1896. (It is now known as the Royal York Hotel.) There is drama inside this unbecoming pile: an elegant staircase rises from the towering central lobby, while above, three levels of iron galleries bridge the stairs. But the most exciting and unexpected feature is down below, near the Station Road entrance.

Descend the almost cramped stairs, and a warm, brown ceramic archway hoves into sight. This is the entrance to the Tiles Bar, which harbours a most magical interior of rich, decorative, late Victorian ceramics.

Apart from the floor, all surfaces are glazed: a massive and shiny brown chimneypiece reaches to the ceiling, tiles in shades of green, yellow and brown cover the walls, while the ceiling itself is a riot of pendulous bosses in yellow and green, dripping from a background of buff circles.

This is the work of the Leeds Fireclay Company, who marketed their wares under the trade-name Burmantofts, and were market leaders in the late nineteenth and early twentieth centuries for these huge, glazed displays, which were most popular in pubs and offices. The Tiles Bar probably dates from 1896, when the towered addition to the Royal Station Hotel was constructed. Happily, it still functions as a bar, and is the perfect spot to end a tour of York, the home of the Railway King.

FENS, CARRS AND COMMONS

Derwent Vale

THE BEATEN track is far away in this least-known margin of the least-known Riding, where the Derwent meanders south through the Vale of York to meet the Ouse. Bounded by North and West Ridings, squeezed between the Wolds and the Humber Estuary, the broad valley of the lower Derwent is the black hole of Yorkshire, crossed by motorway but a mystery to most, with placenames awash with marsh and drain: Saltmarshe and Gilberdyke, Foulness and Yokefleet.

To the north, where the weird undulations of the Wolds almost meet the Derwent, stands Norton, now a substantial settlement in its own right, but once something of a genteel appendage to the market town of Malton, across the river in the North Riding.

On Norton's main thoroughfare, Commercial Street, a green bull's head gazes down from above the doorway of a butcher's shop of most traditional appearance. Cream and green ceramics in Classical style form the façade, whilst inside, colourful tile-panels show more candidates for the chopper enjoying rural contentment. The date was 1912, and all was well with the world at Freer's the family butchers — albeit not for long.

To follow the Derwent south, head back towards Malton but almost immediately turn left at the level crossing; the by-road climbs over Langton Wold, then descends to cross Menethorpe Beck. Bear right soon after the beck to negotiate a narrow lane and regain the river at Kirkham Priory. Here are spectacular ruins in a ravishing, picturesque setting; catch a glimpse from the train, as it passes on the far bank, and Kirkham seems dreamlike, but the reality is a gritty tale of religious argument and financial crisis.

The priory was founded around 1122 by the lord of Helmsley, Walter l'Espec, who went on to establish Rievaulx Abbey in 1131. Initially Augustinian, the house almost turned Cistercian within twenty years, inspired by the success of several new Cistercian foundations in Yorkshire. The hardline Augustinians intended to leave, taking all ornamental finery with them, whilst the remainder felt drawn to the Cistercians; but, in the end, no split occurred, and Kirkham remained Augustinian.

The priory church was built in the twelfth century, but the first half of the thirteenth century saw much rebuilding; financial difficulties duly followed in the fourteenth century, and the construction programme was scaled down. The priory went into debt and the number of canons dropped, although Kirkham survived the fifteenth century in relatively stable condition.

The plan of the priory is easy to make out from the foundation walling, and the most impressive of the ruins is the late thirteenth-century gatehouse, to the north-west of the church. In Decorated style, it boasts heraldic and figurative sculptures, including St George and the Dragon.

Howsham, the birthplace of 'Railway King' George Hudson, is three miles downstream and a little further by road; bear right out of Kirkham and again in Westow, passing the eighteenth century hall, then head down to the river soon after meeting the Norton road. Hudson was born in the village of brown-stone cottages in 1800. He was the son of a farmer, and was apprenticed to a draper in York before an inheritance set him on the path to fortune, then disaster, in the railway boom. The single line of cottages was rebuilt after 1772 when the grounds of Howsham Hall, standing to the north, just above the river, were redesigned as a park, taking in part of the old village. This was possibly the work of 'Capability' Brown.

The magnificent south front of Howsham Hall dates from around 1610, and if not designed by Robert Smythson, is certainly greatly influenced by his style, where soaring façades are dominated by huge windows. The two-storey, grey-stone mansion has a wonderfully decorative parapet topped by ball finials, and windows to spare, but the interior is by another hand; it was reconstructed around 1775 for Nathaniel Cholmley, perhaps by John Carr.

Georgian improvement also extended to the stables, while in the woods to the north of the hall lurks an octagonal tower, and a decorative Gothick watermill (now derelict) lies west of the hall on the river. The mill, also perhaps by Carr, was both functional and folly, a throwback to the romantic ideal of the medieval miller.

The village church, St John the Baptist, was also provided by the Cholmley family, in the person of Hannah Cholmley. It was built in 1859-60 and her chosen architect was George Edmund Street, who had recently published his influential work *Brick and Marble in the Middle Ages*. Although Street occasionally tried his hand at public buildings, he was firstly an ecclesiastical architect, whose early village churches tended to be massive and spare; he introduced polychromy into his designs during the mid-1850s. Howsham is a fine example of this period, combining strength and decoration. A bonus is the stained-glass scheme — commissioned by Street from Clayton & Bell of London when the firm was at its best — using new colours and finely-detailed drawing.

Back on the Norton road, head south for a couple of miles, then turn right to the river and Scrayingham, where there is more good

This green ceramic façade in Classical style was added to the butcher's shop on Commercial Street, Norton, in 1912. Inside are colourful tile-panels showing wholesome cattle.

Clayton & Bell glass in the church of St Peter, and a surprise to be found in the churchyard: the grave of the Railway King lies south of the west end of the church. George Hudson died in 1871, and perhaps his descent to disgrace led to his burial in such unremarkable surroundings.

Follow the river south by road, past the bridge to Buttercrambe where Aldby Park, a fine, early Georgian house, looks across the Derwent from its parkland setting in the North Riding. On to the A166; a couple of miles to the west is Stamford Bridge, site of the defeat of Harold Hardrada, King of Norway, by King Harold of England on the 25th September 1066. Of course, the end came for England's

Harold less than a month later at Hastings. All signs of the battlefield have long since disappeared, including the bridge itself, which for a time divided English and Vikings. It was upstream from the present bridge, which was erected in 1727 by William Etty of York. One of its three arches spans a lock, built when the Derwent Navigation was improved during the first two decades of the eighteenth century.

Stamford Bridge's imposing, water-powered corn mill was built in the eighteenth century to make use of the Derwent as both power supply and waterway. Its main five-storey block, set above the river on a monumental arcade, is an extension dating from the 1820s. Watermills were once common throughout the Riding, although the north and west scarp-slopes of the Wolds were particularly popular locations. The industrialisation of corn milling in the late nineteenth century resulted in the disappearance of many small mills, but some have been converted to new uses; the Stamford Bridge mill closed as recently as 1964, and a waterwheel still remains in the building, which is now a restaurant.

A little further downstream, sixteen arches of a now-disused railway viaduct plod across the fields; there are fifteen brick arches and a main cast iron arch, with a ninety foot span, which straddles the Derwent. The viaduct was part of the York & North Midland line which opened in 1847 and connected York with Market Weighton; it was designed by company engineer John Birkinshaw. The cast iron span is one of the oldest examples of its type still extant.

Below Stamford Bridge the Derwent no longer forms the border between North and East Ridings, but still acts as a barrier to progress; road bridges are infrequent — indeed there are only four possible crossing points on the twenty-three miles of river connecting Stamford Bridge and the Ouse. To explore the flat lands west of the Derwent, head west from Stamford Bridge along the A166, turning south on the York ring road (A64) and leaving on the A19 for the north. Go towards York for around a third of a mile, then take the left turn (B1222), which crosses back over the ring road and descends towards the Ouse.

Past the village of Naburn, the Ouse swings away from the road; almost a mile south, where the river loops back to hug the road, is Naburn Lock. Although the Ouse was navigable up to York in the mid-eighteenth century, with the assistance of the tides, river improvements had been made by York Corporation from the seventeenth century. In 1727 the Ouse trustees, a body of corporation officials, were empowered to collect tolls from users of the river to pay for further improvements, which culminated in the construction of a dam and lock at Naburn in 1757, bypassing a shallow section of river and increasing its depth upstream.

By the early nineteenth century, river conditions allowed a steamboat to run between York and Hull, and the trustees, who could barely afford such luxury, built themselves a banqueting house beside the lock at Naburn in 1823. It cost £2,742 and is not the most memorable of structures, being a plain, stone building with an emphatic door surround, but the trustees must have delighted in using the banqueting room, so close to their thriving navigation.

However, the trustees had neglected their

financial affairs to such an extent that reforms were necessitated during the 1830s. A new, larger, lock was opened in 1888, and was used by 6,765 boats in 1904-5, the peak year for river traffic. A substantial proportion consisted of steam barges carrying grain and flour to and from Leethams flour mill in central York. However, Leethams moved to Hull after the First World War, and the Ouse waterway never regained the heights of its Edwardian prosperity.The road south soon passes Moreby Park, the estate of Moreby Hall, built by Anthony Salvin for Henry Preston in 1828-33. The rambling Tudor-Gothic pile was only the second country house to be designed by Salvin, who eventually became one of the foremost practitioners in this field.

A mile or so further is Stillingfleet and the church of St Helen. Its Norman south doorway flaunts all manner of carved beasts, and the unusual ironwork on the door is something of a mystery, maybe Viking in character. Inside, the Moreby Chapel displays Jacobean screens.

Bear right on leaving Stillingfleet, to follow the Ouse through Kelfield to Riccall, where St Mary offers another excellent Norman south doorway. The church was restored by John Loughborough Pearson during 1862-77.

Take the busy A19 south from Riccall, turning left on to the A63 at Barlby to head for the beckoning spire of Hemingbrough church, another St Mary. The dominance of the glorious spire is emphasised by its positioning on top of a squat tower; 126 feet of spire stand upon 63 feet of tower, giving a total height of 189 feet, in comparison with the mere 148 feet length of the church itself. The body of the building, constructed from white Tadcaster stone, dates mainly from the thirteenth century, but the spire was added by the Prior of Durham in the mid-fifteenth century. Inside St Mary is some fine woodwork, including a misericord which may be the oldest in England, dating from around 1200.

Take the by-road north of Hemingbrough, crossing the A163 and pressing on for a couple of miles across Skipwith Common to Skipwith village. Here, the church of St Helen has stunning Early English ironwork on the south door, and a particularly elegant chancel.

Five miles north-west of Skipwith is Escrick, where we find a rather different church of St Helen. This colourful, urbane building was erected in 1856-7 at the expense of its incumbent, the Reverend Stephen Willoughby Lawley, and local landowner Lord Wenlock, also a member of the Lawley family. Their architect was Francis Cranmer Penrose, surveyor of St Paul's Cathedral, who produced a church in fourteenth century style with Victorian trappings: red and black marble pillars support the brick-vaulted roof of the baptistery at the west end, and a white marble font is held aloft by two cherubs. There is even an unexpected monument by the renowned sculptor and designer Eric Gill, dating from 1907; who else could it commemorate but the Reverend Lawley himself?

Head east from Escrick to Wheldrake, a pleasant village of mainly eighteenth century, brick-built estate houses. A little to the south is Thicket Priory, a red-brick, Tudor-style pile with a skyline full of chimneys, gables and towers. It was built in 1844-7 — close to the site of an old manor house and an even older priory — by antiquarian and architect Edward Blore, then nearing the end of his long career as a specialist in Tudor and

The tower of the Church of St Peter, Howden, seen through the east window of its ruined chancel. The tower, 135 feet in height, was built around the start of the fifteenth century; the chancel collapsed in 1696.

Elizabethan country houses. The mansion became a Carmelite nunnery in 1955. Take the road north from Wheldrake, turning right at the B1228 for Elvington, thence crossing the Derwent on Elvington Bridge.

Keep on the B1228 through Sutton upon Derwent, and cross the restored Pocklington Canal at Hagg Bridge in a couple of miles. The canal was opened in 1818 and ran between the Derwent at East Cottingwith and Canal Head, a point near the main York-Hull road a mile south of Pocklington. The prohibitive cost of constructing extra locks made entry to the town itself impossible. There were nine locks in the course of the nine and a half mile canal, and several steep, hump-backed, brick-built bridges carrying minor roads across the water. Trade along the canal consisted mainly of coal and agricultural produce, and the undertaking was moderately profitable. However, in 1848, the year following the arrival of the York & North Midland Railway Company's line in Pocklington, the same company took over the canal. Traffic gradually diminished and the canal silted up; it was hardly used at all by the time of the First World War, but restoration has been taking place since the 1970s.

A mile east of Hagg Bridge, turn left from the B1228 and follow the line of the canal to Melbourne; here there is a real curiosity, a corrugated iron church which dates from 1882.

A little over three miles to the east is Everingham, where one of the most magnificent pieces of architecture in the Riding, the Chapel of the Virgin and St Everilda, may be found standing in the grounds of Everingham Hall. Huge, Italian chapel faces conservative, Georgian hall, each puzzled at the other's presence beside the neatly-mown lawn.

Red-brick Everingham Hall was built by John Carr for William Haggerston Constable in 1757-64 and enlarged, to over twice its original size, in the nineteenth century. The additions were removed and the Carr hall restored in neo-Georgian style in 1962-3 by Francis Johnson, a Bridlington-based architect who has built in his austere, modern version of the Classical style throughout the North of England. The bulk of the Roman Catholic chapel quite overshadows the polite hall. Its construction in 1836-9 resulted from the passing of the Act of Emancipation in 1829, which legalised the building of Catholic chapels. Previously, most of these were located within private homes, although a separate Classical chapel (since demolished) was added to Houghton Hall, just south of Market Weighton, in 1827-9. Perhaps William Constable-Maxwell, grandson of William Haggerston Constable, intended to outdo his near-neighbour at Houghton; he commissioned the young Italian architect Agostino Giorgioli to produce a design for the chapel, which was carried out by John Harper of York (then working on the original buildings of St Peter's School, Clifton).

The chapel has a severe façade, arched and pedimented, while inside is a richly-decorated rectangular hall, lined by giant Corinthian columns, leading to an apsidal east end (in ecclesiastical terms — it is actually geographical north) which holds the altar. The barrel-vaulted roof is white and gold, while the columns are brown scagliola, an imitation marble. In niches between the columns are statues of the saints, while an image of St Everilda, a Saxon saint said to have founded a nunnery at Everingham, stands in the apse.

The ruins of the chapter house of St Peter in Howden. The octagonal chapter house was built at the end of the fourteenth century, and was the last in the line of such polygonal structures.

All these are by the Italian sculptor Leopoldo Bozzoni, who moved to England to execute this commission in 1839-44.

After the shock of Everingham, head south through Harswell to join the A163 for Holme-on-Spalding-Moor.

Holme means island hill, and just to the east of the town is the church of All Saints, rising high above the main road on isolated Church Hill, where Holme itself probably originated. As most of the Vale of York reaches no more than twenty-five feet above sea level, this lofty vantage point — an outcrop of Triassic mudstone all of 150 feet in height — provides an expansive view. All Saints dates from the thirteenth century onward; the tower is Perpendicular while the brick porch is an eighteenth century addition, but what remains in the mind is not details but the overall impression, of hill, church and especially churchyard.

From Holme, turn south along the A614, crossing flat commons and the River Foulness. A brief deviation to the hamlet of Bursea (take a left turn three miles out of Holme) will lead the traveller to its William Butterfield church of 1870-2, small but typically displaying red and blue brick. The ancient market town of Howden is six miles further, its approach dominated by the tower of St Peter, one of the biggest churches in the East Riding.

The size of St Peter is explained by the relationship between the town and the Bishop of Durham, who was lord of Howdenshire. Howden's markets and fairs included an important horse-fair, granted to the bishop in 1200, and these remained at the centre of its prosperity until the nineteenth century. The church was made collegiate (in that it had a

This market cross, designed in Gothic style and erected in 1909, stands in Market Place, Howden.

college with dean and canons attached to it) in 1267, and was then rebuilt on a massive scale. The nave was completed around 1300, the chancel around 1320, but the crossing tower, 135 feet in height, was still under construction at the start of the fifteenth century. There is also a fine octagonal chapter house, in Perpendicular style with thirty seats, which was built at the end of the fourteenth century but this, like the chancel, lies in ruins (although it has recently been re-roofed).

The magnificent church proved too much for the townspeople to maintain after the Dissolution, and by 1609 services were taking place in the nave, as they do today. Lead from the chancel roof was used to repair the nave, leaving the chancel unstable; it collapsed during a thunderstorm in 1696, and the roof of the neglected chapter house fell in 1750. But together, the picturesque ruins and cathedral-like remains make a splendid spectacle beside the market place.

East of Howden, the B1230 bridges the motorway and crosses the fens, meeting the Market Weighton Canal at Newport, the sole industrial village of the Riding.

There was almost nothing here prior to 1780 except a watery common, but drainage, enclosure and the discovery of good-quality clay during excavations for the canal led to the establishment of brickworks and the growth of the settlement. The nine-mile canal reached from the Humber to a point two miles short of Market Weighton, the cost of actually entering the town being too great, due to the need for extra locks. It was fully opened by 1782, and acted as a drainage channel as well as a navigation. By the 1820s, annual shipments of bricks along the canal amounted to two million, and over half the income of the navigation derived from bricks, tiles, and coal for the brickyards by the mid-nineteenth century. However, the canal was bought by the York & North Midland Railway in 1847 and trade slowly diminished; the last commercial craft used the canal in 1958.

Two roads lead west of Howden; the more southerly is a by-road which leads to Barmby on the Marsh and the junction between Derwent and Ouse, now marked by a tidal barrage which was completed in the late 1970s. To the north, the A63 crosses the Derwent at Loftsome Bridge, where the remains of the first bridge, which replaced a ferry service in 1804, may still be seen in the river. Turn north just before the bridge to reach Wressle and the romantic ruins of Wressle Castle, adrift in the riverside meadows.

The pair of towers and their connecting wall form the only substantial remnant of a castle left in the East Riding. Sir Thomas Percy built Wressle Castle around 1380; it was still in good condition in the 1530s, but had begun to decay later in the century, and was partly demolished on the instructions of Parliament in 1648, to prevent its use by the Royalists. There were originally five towers centred on a courtyard, with a garden and orchard inside a moat, and a pleasure garden to the south. Today there is no sign of the gardens, but the beautiful white stonework and almost domestic scale of the ruins makes Wressle more manor house than castle, a friendly fortification in a gentle landscape.

A HEAP OF MOUNTAINS

The Western Wolds

FOR CENTURIES the landscape of the East Riding has been undervalued. The antiquarian William Camden derided its spine, the chalk Wolds, as 'nothing but a heap of mountains' in his guidebook *Britannia*, published in 1586.

Its weirdly rolling Wolds may not have the immediate impact of the high moors and dales, but to be enfolded in the mazy dry valleys of the Wolds is a memorable experience, one enhanced by occasional architectural reminders of previous inhabitants.

The buildings of the Wolds cannot be understood without reference to the unforgettable Sykes family of Sledmere House. Stand by the gaunt and Gothic monument to Sir Tatton Sykes, perched on Garton Wold by the B1252, nearly three miles south-east of Sledmere, for a fine view over the Wolds and a first taste of the Sykes addiction to building. The Wolds spread out gently to the east, for this is the dip slope of the great chalk crescent of hills, which begins on the coast at Flamborough and ends, in Yorkshire at least, with the Humber Estuary.

The memorial tower, a curious, spiky and very solid affair of red and brown stone, all of 120 feet in height, was erected in 1865 to commemorate the first Sir Tatton, who had died two years before. Its architect, the otherwise unknown John Gibbs of Oxford, was the triumphant winner of a design competition which attracted 156 entries. Perhaps Sir Tatton's son, the second Sir Tatton, chose the obscure Gibbs as a form of revenge on his father, who frequently sent his son on long trips away from home, so as to be temporarily rid of him. The relief on the base of the column shows the first Sir Tatton on horseback, for horses — their racing, breeding and hunting — along with farming and building were his main interests.

The Sykes family involvement with Sledmere began in 1748, and the present house dates from the rebuilding of the original manor house, a medieval structure, by Richard Sykes in 1751. It was enlarged by Sir Christopher

A detail from the relief on the memorial to the first Sir Tatton Sykes, showing the first Sir Tatton, a keen horseman. On another face of the column is an estate scene, with a finely-carved plough standing before a farmstead.

Sykes, with the assistance of the architects John Carr and Samuel Wyatt, during 1784-92; although both architects produced drawings for the house, Sir Christopher ultimately acted as his own architect, and seems to have thoroughly enjoyed the intricate process of designing and building. There were problems, however, which would be familiar to a modern home-improvement enthusiast: in 1789, a handsome set of doors arrived from London complete with hinges, but without the necessary screws.

Sir Christopher's efforts resulted in the addition of two wings to the basic square, stone house. He commissioned the plasterer Joseph Rose, who had worked for Robert Adam, to decorate the interiors, and was still buying furnishings for the house in 1799. The simple but elegant Classical mansion survived until a fire in 1911. Walter Brierley of York carried out the restoration, and added a chapel.

Agricultural improvement was as important as architecture to Sir Christopher; his works on the Sledmere estate began in 1774 with a survey of the parish, which was enclosed after 1776. Lancelot 'Capability' Brown was brought in to advise on landscaping, but once again Sir Christopher pursued his own ideas, and produced a picturesque plan for the estate based on Brown's rather dull layout. Over 1,000 acres of trees were planted, and a series of farmsteads established around the edge of the park. This gave Sir Christopher scope for further architectural enjoyment. Most of the farm buildings were erected to his designs, and they exhibit a fine understanding of the practical needs of a farm, as well as a good eye for pleasurable proportions.

Castle Farm, half a mile north of the B1252,

The memorial to the first Sir Tatton Sykes, erected in 1865 on Garton Wold near Sledmere. The Gothic tower rises 120 feet above the Wold.

A path of setts (small stone blocks) leads to the Church of St Mary at Sledmere. St Mary was built in 1897-8 and stands close to Sledmere House.

and a mile east of the house, was an exception in that it was designed by John Carr as something of an eyecatcher. The site was probably selected when 'the Great Brown' visited Sledmere in September 1777, and building was complete by the autumn of 1778. The farmhouse took the form of an oversize Gothic gatehouse, with a pair of battlemented turrets guarding an arched gateway. It was originally intended as a dower house — one reserved for a widow — and was only used as a farmhouse from the late nineteenth century.

Sir Christopher Sykes died in 1801, leaving behind him a much-improved estate. His memorial is a domed, Tuscan rotunda which shelters the village well; it was erected in 1840 by the first Sir Tatton Sykes, who inherited the estate in 1823. Sir Tatton's building activities were concentrated upon schools, while his son, the second Sir Tatton, spent much of his time and money on the construction and restoration of churches throughout the Sykes estates. He employed the best architects — Hodgson Fowler, Temple Moore and his particular favourite, G E Street — and lavished over £2,000,000 on this ecclesiastical hobby.

The combination of Sir Tatton and Street was responsible for building seven new churches at villages within ten miles of Sledmere during 1868-78. All the churches were fairly small, but Street was able to display his gifts for inventive design and decoration, and no two are the same. The church of St Mary in Sledmere was the work of Temple Moore, who was taken up by Sir Tatton after the death of Street. It was built in 1897-8 and stands in the grounds of the house.

Sir Tatton died in 1913 at the age of eighty-seven, leaving the estates to his son, Sir Mark

The Waggoners War Memorial at Sledmere, which dates from 1919, is memorable for its portrayal of the enemy in retreat (on the bottom left of the central column).

Sykes. Sir Mark travelled widely whilst waiting to inherit, and his visits to the Middle East prompted the installation of a tiled Turkish room in Sledmere House. The room was copied from a Victorian mosque found in Istanbul. Sir Mark did not have the chance to build on such a grand scale as his forbears, but designed a war memorial to his own army company, the Waggoners. Unusually for such a memorial, it features the enemy — in some disarray — as well as the heroic deeds of the home troops. The stumpy, highly- decorated column also turned out to be a personal monument; the death of Sir Mark occurred just before it was erected in the village during 1919.

There are other follies and monuments dotted around the Sledmere landscape, but to see more of the Wolds, head north towards the North Riding border. Leave the village by the narrow road running north-west to Kirby Grindalythe, where the church of St Andrew was restored by Street for Sir Tatton Sykes in 1872-8. It was their last joint effort, as Street died in 1881. Here, his decorative touches include stone inlay on the pulpit, a brass lectern and a delightful gateway to the churchyard. A strange element is the mosaic, portraying the ascension of Christ, which covers the whole of the west wall.

Three more Sykes and Street churches are near at hand. Two miles east along the valley is West Lutton, where St Mary, rebuilt in 1874-5, boasts an unusual tile-hung belfry. Inside, there is an iron screen by Street, and a painted reredos and stained glass in the west window, both by the London firm of Burlison & Grylls. (John Burlison and Thomas Grylls trained with Clayton & Bell, setting up on

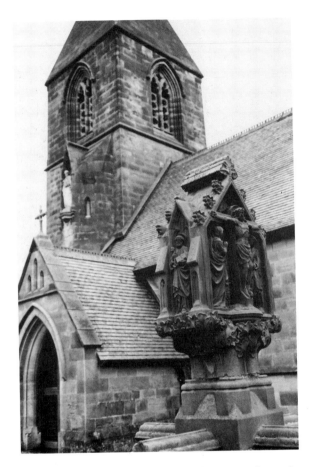

The Church of St Peter stands above the village of Helperthorpe, and was rebuilt by G E Street in 1875. Inside, the nave and chancel roofs are richly painted.

their own account in 1868.) Less than two miles further east is Helperthorpe, where the church of St Peter was rebuilt by Street for Sir Tatton in 1875; Temple Moore added a north aisle in 1893. There is more Burlison & Grylls glass, and an unusual west tower. In Weaverthorpe, just a mile onward, the

The Church of St Andrew at Weaverthorpe. Its tower dates from the early Norman period.

This brass chancel screen formed part of the restoration of the Church of St Andrew carried out by G E Street in 1870-2.

Norman church of St Andrew was restored by Street in 1870-2. One of his new contributions was the iron pulpit, while the altarpiece and stained glass are by Clayton & Bell. An elegant, brass chancel screen completes this fine exhibition of late Victorian craftsmanship, unexpectedly hidden away in the Wolds.

Turn north at Weaverthorpe, and make for the brow of the Wolds; the view over the Vale of Pickering from the northern scarp is excellent. The country lane meets the busy A64 on the valley floor, not far from the River Derwent at Sherburn. A couple of miles east is Ganton, a tiny village dominated by the grounds of Ganton Hall, home of the Legard family until 1911. The original house, probably

Elizabethan, was replaced in 1866-8 by a many-chimneyed, neo-Jacobean mansion in red brick. Since the late seventeenth century, the south transept of the thirteenth to fifteenth century church of St Nicholas has served as the Legard mausoleum. A wooden screen shields the burial vault from the nave.

West of Sherburn, the A64 passes the excellent Sykes and Street church of St Andrew at East Heslerton, built in 1873-7; its picturesque silhouette is enhanced by an octagonal steeple. At West Knapton, a little over three miles further west and just to the north of the main road, the church of St Edmund offers an almost entirely painted interior. It seems to date from restoration during the 1870s, and displays delicate flora and fauna amongst assorted patterns; a fine hammerbeam roof sets off the whole scene.

Continue less than half a mile along the A64 to find the by-road running south to the lonely village of Wintringham, and the impressively large church of St Peter. It dates from Norman times onward, and inside is Jacobean joinery and some fine, late fourteenth century stained glass. Now back to the main road and west. The grounds of Scampston Hall lie immediately to the north, where 'Capability' Brown worked in 1772-3.

At Rillington, turn south on a narrow by-road which passes through Thorpe Bassett before climbing up and over the wold, to reach Settrington on the far side. This estate village owes its present appearance to Sir Mark Sykes of Sledmere House, who acquired the manor of Settrington by marriage in 1795. He quickly rebuilt the Tudor manor house, Settrington House (which was redesigned after a fire in 1963 by Francis Johnson of Bridlington), while his wife Henrietta transformed the village. Limestone cottages replaced timber-framed dwellings in planned formation around the beck. All Saints Church, in happy juxtaposition with the manor house, dates from the twelfth century but has been much rebuilt.

Head south for a couple of miles to North Grimston, on the B1248, where the mainly thirteenth century church of St Nicholas is home to a splendid Norman font. This massive, stone cylinder is carved with a rendering of the Last Supper so detailed that the food on the table is easily visible, if not instantly identifiable. The by-road west of North Grimston leads to the pleasant estate village of Langton, built as an entity in the 1820s and 1830s. At the crossroads half a mile west of Langton, turn south, visiting the tiny settlements of Kennythorpe and Burythorpe before heading east to Birdsall.

The presence of two churches in the village, an abandoned building dating from the Norman period and an estate church built in 1824, reflects the changes wrought in the Wolds by Georgian and Victorian improvers. Near the old church stands Birdsall House, a mid-eighteenth century pile with later additions, including an entire top floor designed by Anthony Salvin in 1872-5. The patron of the new church, St Mary, was the sixth Lord Middleton; his architect was John Oates of Halifax, a church specialist. The church was extended in 1879-81, the new chancel being added by Hodgson Fowler. Lord Middleton's white marble monument may be found inside.

Local farmsteads also benefited from modernisation during the nineteenth and early

The ruined church of St Mary at the deserted medieval village of Wharram Percy.

This extravagant clock resides on the tower of the Church of St Mary, Fridaythorpe; it dates from the restoration of 1902-3.

twentieth centuries: accommodation for stock was upgraded, yards were covered over, and, more recently, sizeable barns and grain silos sprung up to dwarf earlier farm buildings. Altogether, the landscape of the estate farms is almost unrecognisable compared with the pre-enclosure days before the 1690s.

A tiny road runs east of Birdsall to the crossroads at Wharram le Street; here, turn right along the B1248, and shortly right again to find the start of a narrow footpath which leads to the remains of the evocative deserted village of Wharram Percy. The ruined church of St Mary, mainly eleventh to fourteenth century, and with a small, seventeenth century chancel, is one of the more substantial reminders of the past. The village was in decline by the fourteenth century, and the Black Death and enclosure combined to complete its depopulation.

Three miles south of Wharram Percy is Thixendale, hidden amongst the steepest, deepest and eeriest of the dry valleys which make up the Wolds. The village was part of the Sledmere estates between 1793 — when Sir Christopher Sykes became the dominant landowner — and 1941. Its church, St Mary the Virgin, was erected in 1870 for the second Sir Tatton Sykes by G E Street, who also designed the school and vicarage; the three make a pretty composition. Before the building of the new church, the villagers had a bracing walk across the wolds to Wharram Percy to worship.

A couple of miles south-east of Thixendale, over Thixendale Wold, is Fridaythorpe, very much a working village with a Norman church restored in 1902-3 by Hodgson Fowler for Sir Tatton Sykes. There is a highly decorative Norman south doorway, but most noticeable is the sizeable clock perched on the side of the tower, a showy emblem of the restoration.

Leave Fridaythorpe along the A166, heading east through Wetwang, where the Norman church of St Nicholas was restored in 1901-2 by Sir Tatton and Hodgson Fowler, to Garton-on-the-Wolds, where the Sykes influence is again in evidence, at the church of St Michael and All Angels.

The church dates from the eleventh century, although its first substantial building was erected in the twelfth century. Fourteenth and fifteenth century alterations were followed by restoration in 1856-7, carried out by John Loughborough Pearson for the first Sir Tatton Sykes.

After his father's death in 1863, the second Sir Tatton brought in Street to make his mark on the church, which he did between 1872 and 1877, producing a magical, vividly colourful and unique interior.

Clayton & Bell covered the nave and chancel walls with a series of paintings which show the biblical version of the creation and the labours of the months; the latter is a medieval sequence often used to illustrate the signs of the zodiac. Below this frieze Street added a ceramic dado, using Spanish cuenca tiles. These feature high-relief geometric patterns, made by pressing a mould into the tile, with distinctive green, purple, orange and white glazes. Street, who published the standard text *Some account of the Gothic architecture of Spain* in 1869, often used ceramics in his church restorations, a clear reference to the Moorish decoration found in Christian churches in Spain.

Sir Tatton returned to Pearson for the

The creation of Eve, as portrayed in a painting on the north wall of the nave at the Church of St Michael and All Angels, Garton-on-the-Wolds. The series of paintings, which cover the nave and chancel walls, and the tile frieze below were part of the restoration carried out by G E Street for the second Sir Tatton Sykes in 1872-7.

completion of the Garton scheme, perhaps because of Street's time-consuming involvement with the construction of the Law Courts in London. The chancel floor was laid out with coloured marble and mosaic, and stained glass by Clayton & Bell, also designed on the creation theme, was installed in 1879. The overall result was a surprising, exciting and tremendously rich interior. Restoration in 1985-91 has ensured the survival of this incomparable Victorian decorative scheme.

Head south from Garton to meet the A163 near Kirkburn. The mostly-Norman parish church of St Mary has a wonderful font, a massive stone tub with crude and powerful carvings depicting a winged serpent and rather aggressive figures. Take the main road for two miles south-west of the village, then use the B1246 to climb the gentle Wolds slopes, reaching the top of the scarp near the attractive village of Warter.

The relatively undistinguished church of St James at Warter, built in 1862-4, boasts a fine set of early twentieth century monuments, both inside and out. They commemorate members of the Wilson family, Hull shipowners who lived at nearby Warter Priory, a huge French Renaissance-style pile rebuilt in 1872, on the base of a late-seventeenth century house. In the churchyard are a pair of bronzes dating from 1909 and 1910, designed by Gilbert Bayes, while marble and metal figures by George Frampton people the interior. A family chapel was added to the church in 1908, but was demolished in 1966. The family home fared no better; it was demolished six years later. Warter Priory took its name from an Augustinian priory founded in 1132, which stood just beside the church.

Just west of Warter, take the small by-road which loops south of the beautiful parkland of Warter Priory and through Nunburnholme, where the shaft of a fine, figure-carved Saxon cross resides in the church of St James. Bear right at the west end of the village to return to the main road, which runs down the escarpment towards Pocklington, leaving the grounds of Kilnwick Percy Hall to the north; look out for the Greek Revival lodge near the roadside.

The hall has a confused building history, with assorted additions and demolitions, but what remains is a piece of Greek Revival dating from 1845, with a giant Ionic portico. Since 1986 it has functioned as a Buddhist college and holiday centre; the ballroom is now a meditation room, its Classical decoration providing a quaint backdrop for numerous images of Buddha.

In a mile or so, the B1246 descends into the busy little market town of Pocklington, a complete contrast to the loneliness of the Wolds. The town was too close to York to thrive as a main centre; its canal, opened in 1818 and intended to connect Pocklington with the River Derwent, did not even reach the town proper, stopping a mile short. The railway arrived in 1847, at a station designed by G T Andrews for the York & North Midland Railway. Passengers entered and departed beneath an elegant, five-arched Classical colonnade, but since the departure of the railway itself, the converted station has served as a sports hall. In the town centre, a good seventeenth century house has become the Ritz Cinema. The best building in Pocklington is All Saints Church, mainly late twelfth to late thirteenth century in date, but with a tremendous Perpendicular tower.

A by-road runs a mile south of the town to Canal Head, at the junction with the A1079. This was the end point of the Pocklington Canal. Some canalside buildings may still be seen (in various states of repair), including a warehouse, probably built around 1820, and a bone-crushing mill which produced ferti-liser. The mill was powered by steam gener-ated from coal brought in along the canal. There are also wharves, a lock-keeper's cot-tage and an inn.

Head south-east down the main road for nearly two miles, turning off at Hayton to pass through through Burnby; bear right here, and again as the scarp slope rises, to reach the peaceful village of Londesborough which overlooks sweeping parkland to the south.

At first, Londesborough seems a typically splendid Wolds country estate, with pieces of Classical masonry dotted here and there, but it is soon apparent that there is something missing — the great house itself. Londes-borough Hall, the seat of the earls of Burlington, and which for a time during the eighteenth century was home to one of the great powers of English architecture, was demolished as long ago as 1818-9.

The mansion was built in the late seven-teenth century by the first Earl of Burlington; the design was probably based on plans pro-duced in 1676-8 by the scientist and architect Robert Hooke, who worked closely with Sir Christopher Wren. The third earl succeeded to the property in 1704, when aged only ten, and after several visits to Italy became deeply involved with promoting the Palladian archi-tectural style, which was first popular in England almost a century before. During the 1720s and 1730s the third earl, an amateur architect who became the arbiter of English architectural taste, designed a number of seminal buildings in the Palladian style. He died in 1753, and was buried in the family vault at the church of All Saints in Londes-borough.

The house stood above its parkland, look-ing down towards the lake; a terrace remains, where four urns reside upon pedestals, and the cellars are hidden under grass to the rear, south-east of the church. There is also a fine gateway at the south-west corner of the park, probably by Robert Hooke, but that is all. The 12,000 acre estate, minus its house, was sold to the 'Railway King' George Hudson in 1845 for £470,000. The purchase was made partly to block the projected York-Hull route of a rival railway company, and Hudson opened his own York to Market Weighton line, run by the York & North Midland, in 1847. As befits a railway company chairman, he also built himself a private station on the estate, with access to the line.

Back in the village, the expected memorial to the third Earl of Burlington in All Saints Church is simply a small brass plate. No huge architectural conceit, no monumental aspira-tions here, but surely the earl had built memo-rably enough elsewhere. For those of an ar-chitectural turn of mind, the sense of anticli-max engendered by Londesborough — church and estate — is intense, but a stroll through the remaining glories of Londesborough Park may help to suspend one's disbelief that so much has vanished.

Two miles south of Londesborough, in the lee of Goodmanham Wold, stands Market Weighton, a market town which grew up along the main road between York and Beverley, which became a turnpike in 1764. The bypass now removes traffic hurtling through to Hull, leaving in relative peace some buildings of more than passing interest.

All Saints Church dates mainly from the eleventh and thirteenth centuries, but the peculiar brick topping to the tower was added in the late eighteenth century. Close by on the main street is a handsome, five-bay Georgian inn built in red brick, the Londesborough Arms. Its interior is a nightmare for architectural purists, and very enjoyable too; modern materials masquerade as Edwardian Baroque joinery and ceramic barfront. Look for the delightful skylight above the entrance, beyond the Tuscan porch.

The village of Goodmanham lies only a mile north-east of Market Weighton, but well up into the Wolds. The church of All Saints is largely Norman, and boasts an ornate octagonal font, dating from the sixteenth century and thoroughly decorated on almost every surface. In addition an inscription warns that 'With owt baptysm no soull ma be saved'. The old rectory, an elegant, white-brick Greek Revival house now known as Hall Garth, was built in 1823-4 by Charles Mountain of Hull, the city's first neo-Classical architect.Head east of Goodmanham, across the brow of the Wolds, towards the beckoning steeple of St Mary at South Dalton. The church was built in 1858-61 by John Loughborough Pearson for the third Lord Hotham, and stands opposite the gates of Dalton Hall, the Hotham family home.

St Mary is no humdrum estate church, its lavish decoration and 200 foot steeple setting it apart from more mundane places of worship; the stained glass by Clayton & Bell — especially the east window and the rose above it — is outstanding. A monument to Sir John Hotham, who died in 1689, is a gruesome work: a white marble effigy of the man himself lies on a black marble slab, held by four kneeling figures above a similar slab, upon which rests a skeleton.

The pretty almshouses beside the church, erected in 1873 and equipped with a wooden veranda, must have been an ideal spot from which to observe the comings and goings at the hall. The present Dalton Hall is a greybrick, Classical pile, built in 1771-5 and now somewhat altered. Out in the woods to the west of the house is a crusty summerhouse built in the early eighteenth century. Its design, a heavily rusticated arch and pediment covering a central shelter with a room to either side, was well to the fore of architectural fashion at the time, when the Palladian revival was in full swing. It was based on that of the Water Gate at York House in London's Strand, then thought to have been designed by that archetypal Palladian, Inigo Jones, a century earlier.

Returning to Market Weighton, turn south on the Hull road (A1034), running along the lower slopes of the Wolds for a couple of miles to Sancton. The west tower of All Saints Church is unique in the Riding, as it is octagonal from top to bottom.

The local great house, Houghton Hall, lies about a mile to the west; it was built around 1765 for Philip Langdale, and was probably designed by Thomas Atkinson, one of Yorkshire's leading Georgian architects. The main building is small, brick-built and only five bays wide, but it is linked to a pair of three bay pavilions. In 1827-9 Charles Langdale added a Roman Catholic chapel to the house; this was the work of Joseph Ireland from Wakefield, who was himself a Catholic. Ireland's architectural commissions, in a career which lasted from 1808 until the 1830s and took him well away from Yorkshire, tended to come from a clientele of the same faith, and often involved the design of chapels and churches. Unfortunately, his Greek Revival chapel at Houghton was demolished in 1959, when several alterations were made to the house.

Two miles south of Sancton, and lying just above the main road in a valley of Newbald Wold, is the village of North Newbald and the superb Norman church of St Nicholas. There are four excellent doorways — entering the nave, and rather oddly, the transepts, from north and south — the best on the south of the nave. Although the chancel is a product of fifteenth century rebuilding, the crossing is untouched, with four fine Norman arches.

To the south-west, along a by-road which crosses the main road at South Newbald, is Hotham Hall, its village, parkland and church. The original hall was built around 1720 using brown, brick-shaped blocks of local limestone, a contrast to the material most often used in the East Riding for contemporary houses, the ubiquitous brick. A three-bay, pedimented pavilion was added to the house in the eighteenth century, and further extensions followed in the Victorian period.

The park stretches almost a mile south to the village of North Cave on the B1230; follow this road back to the main Hull road to pass Castle Farm, erected in the late eighteenth century as a crenellated eyecatcher for the hall. Most improved Georgian farmstead buildings were strictly plain and functional, however, and even Castle Farm has now lost its battlements.

Motorway and trunk road now approach, but to stay in the Wolds a little longer, remain on the B1230 and head east towards Walkington, turning right soon after the brow is crossed, down a by-road which passes through Little Weighton before reaching Skidby. At the end of this journey is a fine sight, Skidby Mill, the only windmill in Yorkshire to retain its sails. Not only is it complete, it is of a particularly elegant design, with a seven-storey brick tower which is slightly concave in cross-section. A balcony, at four-storey height, allowed the miller to adjust the shutters on the sails according to wind strength. The mill was built in 1821, when windmills were commonplace, but now stands unique on its hill, a great landmark.

Return west over the Wolds, bearing left in Little Weighton — look out for the chalk-built cottage beside the pond — and progress around Rowley village. The odd deviation in the road's line is due to the aspirations of Rowley's early eighteenth century vicar, who built himself a grand rectory (now an hotel) and landscaped the grounds; the road follows the edge of his splendid garden. Bear right at the next junction and head west through the remains of Riplingham, a deserted medieval village, to cross Cave Wold and meet the A1034 at South Cave.

The township, now something of a commuter village, was once a thriving market centre. Its market hall, erected in 1796, still remains as a reminder of South Cave's original function, but the most interesting building is Cave Castle.

This jolly little Gothic castle dates from 1804, and was put up for H B Barnard. The unlikely design, with assorted turrets and battlements carried out in yellow brick, was the work of Henry Hakewill, who specialised in such structures but normally built in the south of England; he later became architect to Rugby School. As the gardens of Cave Castle had earlier been landscaped by a southern gardener, perhaps the whole extravaganza may simply be ascribed to one-upmanship on the part of Barnard. The house was altered in 1875, when the curious gateway was added, and was partly demolished in the 1930s, but the remains are distinctly enjoyable.

From the west end of South Cave, a by-road leads south over the A63 into Ellerker, then back over the trunk road into Branting-ham, an estate village chiefly memorable for the First World War memorial which dominates its centre. Good looks and elegance were not to the fore when this hulk was formed with spare chunks of masonry rescued from the demolition of Cuthbert Brodrick's Italianate town hall in Hull, which was built in 1862 and replaced by the guildhall

Welton House, in the village of Welton, during the early twentieth century. The mansion, now demolished, was the home of the Raikes family.

during 1906-14. The urns which appear around the village emanate from the same source.

All Saints Church, which lies north of Brantingham at the head of a wooded dale, was rebuilt in 1872 by G E Street for Christopher Sykes, who owned the village for a time. Sykes, brother of the second Sir Tatton Sykes of Sledmere, also rebuilt Brantingham Thorpe, the great house to the south of the village. The Elizabethan-style remodelling took place in 1868-82 and was carried out by the prolific country-house architect George Devey. His rambling, picturesque designs often included local materials in an attempt to give new or reconstructed houses the impression of having evolved in the local landscape.

A pleasant walk of a little over two miles connects Brantingham and Welton, to the south-east (leave by the lane heading east — this is part of the Wolds Way), but a journey by road might take in another peculiar miniature castle, this time at Elloughton, back across the A63. It stands in Sands Lane, was built in 1886, and its turrets are covered in stucco; seaside modernism half a century before its time.

There is rather more serious architecture in Welton. Walkers will approach the village down Welton Dale from the north, passing mill and stream before reaching the green and its nineteenth-century stone pump. The area around Welton was enclosed during the latter part of the eighteenth century, and by 1796 wealthy Hull merchants were building fine houses in the village. The best remaining house is stone-built Welton Grange, which dates from around 1741, although Welton Hall and Welton Manor are both decent, late eighteenth century pieces of architecture. The church, St Helen, was thoroughly restored by Sir George Gilbert Scott in 1862-3, and features glass designed by William Morris in six windows, dating from 1877 to 1898.

There is one important house missing from present-day Welton: the home of the Raikes family from Hull. They reconstructed Welton House around 1820, although it was rebuilt again around 1890, before demolition in the mid-twentieth century.

However, the Raikes wisely left a more permanent memorial than a mere residence; a stroll north of the village, to the wooded head of Welton Dale, leads to the site of their mausoleum, hidden (inaccessibly) up in the trees to the left. The circular, domed Raikes Mausoleum was built in 1818 and is decorated with Doric pilasters and a few relief sarcophagi. The delightful little dry valley, typical of the Wolds landscape, and with its surprising but understated architectural element, epitomises the quiet beauty of this underestimated corner of the Riding, so near to the city, yet so very far away.

FROM BRIGG TO BRIDLINGTON

The Eastern Wolds

THE VIEW of Filey from the Brigg is an English seaside classic, and one which has barely changed over more than a century. Gleaming white terraces rise above the water, small boats potter on the water around the coble landing, and promenaders make their way between the little resort and the craggy, coralline promontory across grassy clifftops. Not too much has changed in Filey since the early days of its development as a select seaside resort in the mid-nineteenth century.

There is more to the town than New Filey, the resort; fishermen were working out of the old village of Filey as early as 1120, and the settlement grew up around Church Ravine, which separates the present town from its church, sited to the north of the ravine. An iron-balustered footbridge, built in 1871, crosses the ravine at the end of Church Street and leads into the churchyard of St Oswald. Construction of this impressive building took only about fifty years around the end of the twelfth century. It was owned by the priory at

The Church of St Oswald at Filey.

Bridlington, eleven miles to the south, which supplied priests for church services.

Filey was granted a Friday market in 1221, but the community was never particularly wealthy; agriculture, fishing, and the allied trades of boat-building and rope-making were the main sources of employment. Seaweed was gathered and burned to make kelp, used for its soda, and shipwrecks provided occasions for profitable entertainment. By 1801, soon after the first visitors had discovered the nascent resort, the population was only 505.

Like many other resorts in the early nineteenth century, Filey initially provided almost nothing in the way of facilities for its visitors. Accommodation could be found at either the Ship or Pack Horse inns, and by 1828 there was a choice of two bathing machines on the beach.

The churchyard of St Oswald, Filey. The churchyard runs east from the church towards the cliffs above the coble landing; the coralline mass of Filey Brigg lies half a mile to the north.

This family memorial in Victorian Gothic style can be found towards the east end of the churchyard of St Oswald, Filey.

The impetus for the development of New Filey, south of the original village and facing the sea, came from a Birmingham solicitor, John Wilkes Unett, who from 1835 began buying land, laying out plots and building houses in an area based around the Crescent, the centre-piece of the resort. It was 1890 before the Crescent was complete. By this time, the separation between old and new towns had ended, as the streets running from one to the other were built up.

The six white-stuccoed blocks of the Crescent were constructed by a number of architects and builders, all of whom used variations on a conservative, Classical, domestic style. The most northerly block was put up in

An elegant, early-Victorian ironwork balcony running along an entire block in the Crescent, Filey. Its main decorative motif, leaf-like and fan-shaped, is known as a palmette.

A Greek Doric doorcase in the Crescent. This house was part of the earliest section of the Crescent to be built, and was completed in the 1840s.

1850-1, while the next, standing between Rutland Street and Brooklands, was the first of the Crescent terraces to be built. It was completed in the early 1840s, and exhibits a fine, cast iron balcony — continuous along the entire length of the block — and Greek Doric porches.

Just in Brooklands itself is the unusual Catholic church of St Mary, opened in 1906. The harsh, red-brick building was designed by its first priest, Father E Roulin, who spent the following two decades on decorating the interior; much of the stone carving and joinery was carried out by local craftsmen.

On the beach at Filey between the wars; in the distance is the Brigg, while canvas beach huts dominate the foreground.

Return to the Crescent and walk south, passing the third in the series of stuccoed blocks; this originally consisted of six boarding houses. The next is the Royal Crescent Hotel, built in 1853 by J W Unett. It was central to Unett's development plan for the resort, and provided Filey's most stylish accommodation. With the completion of the remainder of the Crescent, the little resort came to represent a miniature version of Brighton on the East Coast. Filey never attempted to compete with the more popular resorts, and its select tone helped to ensure a longer-term future.

West of Filey, the A1039 hugs the bottom of the Wolds escarpment, first passing through the village of Muston; most of the houses here

date from the eighteenth or nineteenth century, while the church of All Saints, rebuilt in 1863-4, has a pretty double bellcote. Hunmanby, just over a mile to the south, is a large village lying at the foot of the scarp. Its great house, Hunmanby Hall, overlooks the settlement from parkland on the slopes to the west, where a Norman motte-and-bailey castle once stood.

The brick-built hall was erected for the Osbaldeston family in the seventeenth century, although it has been much altered since, particularly during the period between 1928 and about 1990, when the hall was used as a school and several sizeable new buildings were added in the grounds. The park gate, on the southern edge of the village near the station, was built for Humphrey Osbaldeston around 1809 as a sham ruin in the form of a Gothic archway. The building stone was taken from Filey Brigg, despite local protests; however, this was a relatively common occurrence — the Brigg provided stone for Filey's sea wall and Bridlington's piers — and the Brigg survived the frequent attacks on its substance surprisingly well.

The low cliff-top to the east of the village, above Hunmanby Sands, was chosen in 1939 by Bill Butlin as the site of his third holiday camp, following Skegness and Clacton. Construction of the Filey camp was delayed by the onset of war, and the buildings were eventually finished by the government, then used by the RAF for training purposes. The camp opened to the public in 1945, after the grey-painted chalets had been redecorated and the parade ground dug up, to be replaced by a boating lake. Camp architecture at Butlins neatly combined a touch of Modern Movement styling with the concept of the huge, serviced shed, a necessity for the numbers involved in activities, around 9,000 at Filey. Although the camps had no architectural pretensions, they provided a painless introduction to modern design for the public at large, and led to greater acceptance of Modern Movement architecture at the seaside, if not elsewhere. Filey holiday camp, which had its own railway station, was closed in 1983.

Head north-west from Hunmanby village, crossing a low corner of the Wolds to bear left on to the A1039 near Folkton; in a mile or so, turn south to climb back up the scarp on a narrow road which leads to the hamlet of Fordon, hidden away in a remote, but pretty,

dry Wolds valley. The church, St James, is a tiny, stone structure, just a nave and chancel, dating from Norman times. There have been at least two restorations; the most recent, in 1876, accounts for the chancel arch and probably the east window. South-east of Fordon is the trough of the Wold Valley, created by the Gypsey Race, which finds its way to the sea at Bridlington. On the north bank of the stream stands Burton Fleming; the church of St Cuthbert is basically Norman, but with many later alterations. Chapel became more influential than church in the village, however, which saw Wesleyan and Primitive Methodist chapels erected by the mid-nineteenth century. The Wesleyan chapel was rebuilt, using polychromatic brick, in 1883, while a new, red-brick Primitive Methodist chapel was erected in 1903; both stand in Front Street.

The road west of Burton Fleming follows, roughly, the course of the Gypsey Race. About a mile from the village, at a sharp bend to the right, look south to see a massive, tree-covered burial mound, probably late Neolithic in date and known as Willy Howe. Neolithic peoples settled in the Wolds between 4000 and 2000 BC, clearing the scrub and woodland for cultivation and grazing land. The mound, 24 feet high and 130 feet across, has been excavated, but nothing was found in its grave pit.

Further west, and upstream along the Gypsey Race, is Wold Newton, where All Saints Church has a good south doorway dating from the mid-twelfth century. Up on the Wolds, almost a mile south-west of the village and past Wold Cottage, is a stone monument which marks the spot where a meteorite, weighing 561 pounds, fell in 1795. The stone was erected four years later by the owner of Wold Cottage, Edward Topham.

West of Wold Newton, the by-road rises to meet the B1249 just south of Foxholes, worth a visit if only to see the church of St Mary, described by Pevsner as 'one of the ugliest churches in the Riding'. It was completely rebuilt in 1866 in Neo-Norman style, to the design of G Fowler Jones, and actually has quite an enjoyable interior, with a colourful dado of Minton tiles in the chancel.

At Octon crossroads, just over two miles south of Foxholes, turn left along the B1253, bearing left for Thwing after a mile and a half, near the site of Octon village. Until the fifteenth century Octon was a substantial hamlet, but most of its cottages and the chapel of St Michael are now no more than a collection of hefty earthworks. Thwing, unusually for a Wolds village, lies on high ground, and at the junction of six roads. The village church, All Saints, was heavily restored in 1900, but there are remnants from earlier days, notably the decorative, twelfth-century south doorway.

On leaving Thwing, take the by-road which runs south, crosses the B1253 then rolls over the Wolds and down to the large village of Kilham, in a shallow valley formed at the junction of two streams.

Kilham was granted a market and fair in 1227, and its position between the high Wolds to the north and west, and lowlands to the south and east, ensured good agricultural trading, at least until the eighteenth century. The western part of the village, West End, was probably extended due to the initial success of the market. However, the opening of the Driffield Navigation in 1770, which im-

proved the connection between Great Driffield and the Humber Estuary, exacerbated the decline of Kilham as a trading centre, although local merchants had supported the cutting of the canal.

Modern Kilham displays a good collection of domestic buildings, and All Saints Church occupies a prominent position in the centre of the older, eastern part of the village. It is basically a Norman church, but the tower is early fifteenth century and the airy chancel dates from the late thirteenth century. The building was in a poor structural state by the end of the sixteenth century; repairs and alterations have been almost a continuous process since 1818, when a gallery (since removed) was added to the nave. The chancel restoration of 1927 included an east window designed by Kempe & Co.

At Langtoft, three miles to the north-west on the B1249 (bear right after West End), there is earlier glass by the same firm in the church of St Peter, which was restored by Hodgson Fowler for Sir Tatton Sykes of Sledmere in 1900-3. The church is also home to a fine Norman font, removed from Holy Trinity Chapel at the deserted village of Cottam, deeper into the Wolds and about two miles south-west of Langtoft. Cottam was once half the size of Langtoft, but now there is just an excellent set of earthworks and the ruins of the red-brick chapel, which replaced the original around 1890.

Take the B1249 for five miles south from Langtoft, sliding gently down to the edge of the Wolds and meeting the River Hull at Great Driffield, a substantial market town. Little Driffield, a mile to the west, was of some importance in the Middle Ages, but Driffield

Looking north along Market Place, Driffield, in the early twentieth century.

itself grew much more rapidly, eventually acquiring a market, and in trading terms outdoing Kilham to the north. The opening of the Driffield Navigation, which took only three years to complete from the passing of its Act of Parliament in 1767, helped its merchants and markets, while the arrival of the railway in 1846 completed the picture of a healthy market and industrial centre.

Architecturally, the basic appearance of the town has changed little since the Georgian and Victorian period of prosperity, although modern, anodyne shop-fronts have diminished the townscape. Industrial buildings cluster around the canal head, south of the station; the navigation comprised five miles of canal, roughly following the course of the River Hull between Driffield and its junction with Frodingham Beck, and five miles of improvements to the Hull itself. Although

A pair of late eighteenth-century warehouses overlooking the canal, at the head of the Driffield Navigation on the southern edge of Great Driffield.

it was a successful development, the railway proved too competitive, and after a long decline in traffic, the canal saw its final commercial use in the 1940s. The remaining buildings at Driffield include warehouses dating from the 1780s and 1790s, most now converted for residential use, and elegant, nineteenth century cranes.

Aside from industrial archaeology, Driffield can offer All Saints Church, with a splendidly decorative tower which reaches the height of 110 feet. It dates from the fifteenth century, although the body of the church is earlier, mostly early thirteenth century. The voice of dissent provides an impressively competitive structure, the Wesleyan chapel of 1880; unfortunately, the visual impact of the giant Ionic columns supporting its porch has been reduced by intrusive glazing. More to the point is the pleasing general effect provided by the mixture of eighteenth to early twentieth century inns and shops in Driffield's working townscape.

Just a couple of miles to the east is Nafferton, in many ways a smaller version of Driffield, with remains of agriculture-based industries and yet another All Saints Church, which dominates the centre of the village. The earliest parts of its structure date from the twelfth century, but additions were made throughout the centuries — the tower is probably fifteenth century — and several restorations have confused the issue even further.

Not far from All Saints, and still well within the village, is a large pond, beside which once stood a massive maltings, in use until 1966 but since demolished. In a maltings, barley is transformed into malt, an essential raw material for brewing beer. The grains of barley are first soaked in water, then allowed to germinate until their growth is halted by drying in a kiln; the end product is known as malt. In a traditional floor maltings, the grains are spread on the floor to germinate at a controlled temperature, and turned by hand for consistency. More modern maltings achieve germination by putting the wet grains in drums or boxes, with mechanical turning systems; this process, known as pneumatic malting, needs far less floor-space than traditional malting.

The Nafferton maltings was built in 1840 to combine the functions of maltings — common in this barley-growing area — and water-powered corn mill, and took advantage of the Driffield Navigation for transport. The huge maltings, with its vast floors, rose six stories above the village pond. Fortunately, the equally substantial Station Mills, a steam-powered mill erected around 1860 on the southern edge of Nafferton, still stands, close to the railway station. It was rebuilt and much enlarged in 1878, when it also functioned as a maltings, but went over to roller-grinding flour in 1890.

Steam mills and maltings were once ubiquitous in this part of the Riding, but electricity, improved transportation and centralisation in the food industry brought the end of many mills. Floor maltings, with their tremendous space requirements, might have been replaced by the industrialised system of pneumatic maltings during the late nineteenth century, had the brewing industry been more prosperous; in fact, many local floor maltings, with their rhythmic pattern of windows, survived until the mid-twentieth century, when brewing became mainly the province of a few large concerns.

Head north out of Nafferton, joining the A166 as it runs towards Bridlington. After just over a mile, a gentle climb and descent of the edge of Nafferton Wold, turn right at the crossroads for Lowthorpe, to see a weird monument in the church of St Martin. A church has stood in the tiny hamlet since at least the eleventh century, but it was greatly enlarged after 1333 when the patron, local landowner John of Heslerton, made it collegiate. Six priests were at first allocated to the college, which endured until its dissolution in 1548.

The bulk of the church building appears to date from the mid-fourteenth century, but the

All Saints Church at Great Driffield. The fifteenth century tower rises 110 feet above the market town.

An unusual fourteenth-century monument in the Church of St Martin at Lowthorpe, near Great Driffield. The recumbent figures are enfolded in a tree, whose fruits are the heads of children.

once-imposing chancel is ruined and truncated. The latter was probably a result of post-dissolution fears regarding the presence of such an impressive church, while ruination followed around the late eighteenth century. However, the remainder of the church was restored in the mid-nineteenth century.

In the church, originally in the chancel, is a strange and unnerving monument: a tree wraps its branches tightly over and around the stone figures of a recumbent man and woman. Weirder still, thirteen of these growths swell at their ends, each forming the head of a small child, as if fruit, ready to be plucked. In elaboration, the tree roots are transformed into shields. This most gruesome of family trees, dating from the fourteenth century, probably shelters the body of Thomas Heslerton. One hopes the inhabitants are comfortable.

Hurry away; on through Lowthorpe, bearing left in the village to cross the beck and head north to Harpham. Near the church, St John of Beverley, is the site of the manor house owned by the St Quintin family, lords of the manor since the thirteenth century.

There has been a church in Harpham since the early twelfth century, but only a few Norman features remain after rebuilding in the fourteenth century. The main fruits of this process were the fine tower and the memorable St Quintin Chapel, the latter presumably erected around 1349, the date of the earliest monument, the alabaster tomb-chest of William St Quintin. There is also an outstanding brass, showing four foot high figures of Thomas St Quintin and his wife, and other St Quintin memorials which take their family history into the eighteenth century. Even the

stained glass proffers arms of members of the family.

Return to the A166, only a half mile north of Harpham, and head east to visit Burton Agnes and one of the great houses of the Riding, indeed of Yorkshire, Burton Agnes Hall. But first to the old manor house, which stands between church and hall.

In the late twelfth century, Roger de Stutville was lord of Burton Agnes, before it passed via the Somerville family to the Griffiths in 1355. It is probably to Roger de Stutville that we owe the presence of that rarity, a Norman manor house, in the village. Although it was altered in the fifteenth century and the exterior was rebuilt in brick during the seventeenth century, internally it is genuine Norman work, built around 1170-80. In the vaulted undercroft, huge, round, stone piers rise to the roof, supporting the hall above, which is reached by a spiral stair. The low undercroft, its massive stonework lurking in the gloom, is a particularly romantic spot.

Now for the hall, with its marvellous red-brick façade and tremendous glinting, bulging, bow windows, reaching up all of three storeys. It was built in 1601-10 for Sir Henry Griffith, and its design was based on a plan by Robert Smythson, the leading country-house architect of the time. The splendid south façade is heavily fenestrated with a mixture of bows and bays, and the skyline is typically picturesque; gables, chimneys and assorted finials attract the eye upward.

Inside, there is much splendid woodwork and an unusual chimneypiece in the great hall, but the glory of the house is the south-facing long gallery, which originally stretched

Huge columns in the undercroft of the old manor house at Burton Agnes. Climb the spiral stair to the hall above for a fine view of Burton Agnes Hall.

The gatehouse of Burton Agnes Hall, viewed from the gardens to the south of the hall. It was built in 1610, as the hall was being completed.

across the whole of the second floor, a length of 115 feet. Its ceiling is a highly-decorative plaster tunnel-vault, restored from the 1950s after its collapse in 1810 and the consequent subdivision of the gallery.

Sir Henry Griffith died in 1654, and the hall passed into the Boynton family. Celia Fiennes visited her cousin, Sir Griffith Boynton, at Burton Agnes in 1697, and remarked that 'there is a noble gallery over all with large windows on the sides, and at each end painted very curiously, out of which you view the whole Country round'. Sir Griffith made several alterations to the hall, notably decorating the Chinese room, which is lined with screens of painted lacquer.

To the south of the hall is the gatehouse, no mere lodge but a three-storey structure with twin ogee-capped, octagonal towers and an imposing coat of arms, that of James I; this splendid invitation to the house dates from 1610.

To the west stands the church of St Martin, built around 1125-50 to replace an even earlier church. Alterations and additions were made to the fabric up to the early sixteenth century, then the chancel was completely rebuilt in 1730 and other repairs were carried out in the nineteenth century. Amidst the results of this complicated construction history is a fine collection of monuments to members of the Griffith and Boynton families. Sir Henry Griffith, builder of the hall, and his two wives have a chilling and unforgettable tomb-chest covered with sundry sculpted

Bulging, bow windows on the spectacular south façade of Burton Agnes Hall. The huge area of glass is a trademark of the hall's architect, Robert Smythson.

On the outer façade of the gatehouse at Burton Agnes Hall, above the archway, is the coat of arms of James I, flanked by a pair of allegorical figures. The figures were a favourite of the hall's owner, Sir Henry Griffith.

bones and skulls, upon which rest three black coffins.

Back in the daylight, take the by-road north over the Wolds across Wold Gate — a higher-level Roman road which runs west from Bridlington — to All Saints Church at Rudston; here a less forbidding grave may be found,

The monolith at All Saints Church, Rudston. Inside the church is an extravagant reredos of stone and Minton tiles, dating from 1869; most of the stained glass is modern, as the nineteenth century glass was destroyed during the Second World War.

tallest in Britain. This is the Rudston Monolith; it is almost twenty-six feet high, and its base measures six feet across at its widest. The stone was probably brought to the site in the early Bronze Age, about 4,000 years ago, and seems to have originated from Cayton Bay, ten miles distant on the coast near Scarborough. This difficult journey was undertaken because Rudston seems to have been something of a spiritual centre at the time; there are earthworks nearby, including the prehistoric Argam Dikes. This five-mile embankment runs north from just east of Rudston to Reighton, near the coast.

Naturally, the Devil has taken the blame for throwing the monolith at the church. He is notoriously inaccurate with his missiles, although at Rudston he missed by only a matter of four yards; in addition, he was around 3,000 years too early. The first church was built on the site by the early twelfth century, and Norman masonry is still visible in the lower part of the tower, but most of the structure dates from a combination of the thirteenth and fourteenth centuries, and a restoration in 1861.

Only a mile east of Rudston, along the B1253, is Thorpe Hall, a pleasant, early eighteenth to nineteenth century mansion with a park lying to the south-east. There is an unusual collection of ornamental but agricultural outbuildings in the park, mostly dating from the early nineteenth century: an orangery, kennels and stables, an octagonal game larder constructed of timber and, most importantly, a dairy. This, too, is octagonal, was probably built in 1821, and its cool interior is tiled throughout. There are elegant marble tables around the walls, and the central table

that of novelist Winifred Holtby, who recreated the East Riding in her *South Riding*, published in 1936, a year after her death.

Both grave (at the west end of the churchyard) and church are overshadowed by the presence of an enormous standing stone, the carries a marble bowl. Of course, dairies were a normal estate building type, but delicately-decorated dairies became briefly fashionable during the early nineteenth century as adjuncts to country houses; they were often seen as the province of the lady of the house.

The little village of Boynton lies two miles east of Thorpe Hall, in the valley of the Gypsey Race. Its main street runs at right angles to the B1253, and at its southern tip is the church of St Andrew, standing almost next to the gates of Boynton Hall.

Until 1951 the hall was the home of the Strickland family, the dominant influence in the village since the purchase of the manor of Boynton by William Strickland in 1549. Either William Strickland or his son Walter built Boynton Hall in the latter part of the sixteenth century. It was an H-shaped mansion of brick, red with dark blue diapers, and was altered around 1700 when the entrance was moved to a central position; internally, the fine oak joinery and rich plasterwork also date from this period. Lord Burlington produced a plan for further changes in the 1730s, and some work was carried out, but not entirely to his designs. Finally, John Carr was called in during 1765-80 to make more alterations for Sir George Strickland. The result of all this activity was a homely, three-storey mansion of brick and stone, with a fine Venetian window adorning the south front.

Sir George was not content with remodelling his domestic quarters, however; he Gothicised the little, red-brick summer-house which had stood in the park since the sixteenth century, built an ornamental bridge over the Gypsey Race, and erected a water-powered woollen factory just a quarter mile east of the hall, to create employment for the local poor. At one time around over 150 people worked in these Classical surroundings, but by 1770 less than twelve remained, although the building itself still stands.

Sir George's greatest contribution to the Boynton landscape was the construction in 1770 of the Classical eyecatcher known as Carnaby Temple, a mile to the south of the hall. Its design, perhaps by Carr, was based on the Tower of the Winds in Athens, a popular Georgian model. It is a two-storey, octagonal, red-brick conceit with an ogee roof, upon which rests a lantern in the form of a miniature of the temple, topped by a ball final. The windows have been blocked up, giving it a slightly dismal air, but its situation, on a small summit amidst open, rolling fields, makes the journey from Boynton thoroughly worthwhile. The temple stands on a bridleway connecting the Wold Gate by-road with Temple Lane (leading into Carnaby village); it is also visible from the B1253 east of Boynton. Back in Boynton, St Andrew's Church has a chancel packed with monuments to the Strickland family; before modifications to the church in 1910, the chancel served as the family chapel. The church itself was rebuilt for Sir George Strickland by John Carr in 1768-70, although Carr's tower was never built, and the fifteenth century version still adjoins the Georgian body of the church. Another oddity is the double chancel arch. The Strickland family pew was inserted into the tower at gallery level, and as the entrance to the remodelled church was through the medieval tower, the congregation symbolically passed beneath the family on its way to worship.

Rather than rushing directly to Bridlington

and the coast via the B1253, take the by-road north from Boynton to Grindale, thence crossing the railway line to meet the B1229 at its junction with the A165 near Reighton. Now the waters of Filey Bay are only a mile away. Head east along the B1229 towards Flamborough, in three miles passing close to Buckton Hall, standing in isolation between road and cliff top. The manor of Buckton was in the hands of the Robinson family from 1617, and the hall was built by John Robinson in 1744-5. In its original state, the hall was a four-storey Baroque composition with pavilions to either side, but a fire in 1919 gutted the interior and resulted in the replacement of the pitched roof with a flat roof. But the main façade retains good detailing, and part of the monumental garden wall still stands.

A mile or so further east is Bempton, where the church of St Andrew has an unusual wooden screen, topped by the royal arms, in place of the expected chancel arch. Henry Broadley, Hull merchant and lay rector of Bempton, rebuilt the chancel of his medieval church in 1829, and the screen probably dates from the time of this endeavour. As lay rector and owner of the great tithes, Broadley was responsible for maintaining the chancel.Now for Flamborough, marooned on the chalk triangle of Flamborough Head by the sea to north and south, and Danes Dyke to the west. The B1229 crosses the massive earthwork just over a mile out of Bempton, where the road bends right then left, beginning its descent into Flamborough. The embankment, nearly three miles long and reaching over eighteen feet in height, has a deep ditch along its western front, and was probably constructed during the time of the Anglian invasions in

the fifth century, although whether by attacking Angles or defending Britons, it is now impossible to tell.

The manor of Flamborough was held by the Constable family, originally from Chester, from Norman times until 1537, when it was forfeited to the Crown after the execution of Sir Robert Constable; he had been involved in the Pilgrimage of Grace, the Northern rebellion of 1536. The Constables built themselves a fortified manor house just north of the church during the fourteenth century, but all that remains above ground of this substantial structure is part of a square chalk tower. The Constables petitioned the crown and eventually regained their manor, but sold it to Sir Henry Griffith of Burton Agnes in 1636. It was bought in 1650 by a distant member of the Strickland family of Boynton.

Monuments in the church of St Oswald reflect this changing ownership, and include the tomb-chest of Sir Marmaduke Constable, who died in 1520; it has an inscription running to twenty-six lines of verse which relates the stirring deeds of the good knight. The church itself originated with a small Norman building, much enlarged in the thirteenth century, heavily restored in the seventeenth century and rebuilt during 1864-9.

The fine Perpendicular rood-screen and loft, by the Ripon school of wood-carvers, have survived these changes, albeit with some restoration. The loft, a gallery over the partition separating nave and choir, is one of only two remaining in Yorkshire; the other is at Hubberholme in Wharfedale. The Flamborough loft was probably removed from the priory at Bridlington after the dissolution.

Fishing has been important to Flamborough

The old lighthouse at Flamborough Head, a chalk-built octagonal structure dating from 1674. It was erected by the lighthouse entrepreneur Sir John Clayton, but was never lit due to lack of funds.

The new lighthouse at Flamborough Head, which was erected in 1806. The elegant, white tower was designed by Samuel Wyatt of Trinity House, and cost £8,000.

since medieval times, and the settlement was a significant port between the fourteenth and sixteenth centuries. However, there are hardly any buildings remaining which date from before the eighteenth century, and gradual growth during the nineteenth century resulted in a relatively modern appearance for this ancient settlement.

The cliffs and offshore rocks of Flamborough Head, almost two miles east of the village, have always been a hazard to shipping. A lighthouse was first built on the headland in 1674 by Sir John Clayton, who built five lights — the others were in Norfolk, Suffolk and Northumberland — in an unsuccessful attempt to make a profit from shipping tolls. At Flamborough, a voluntary toll on passing ships proved inadequate, and the octagonal, chalk tower was never lit. The sturdy, eighty foot tower still stands, about half a mile inland from the Head, to the north of the road from the village. The building economically combined the function of lighthouse and dwelling for the light-keeper.

Between 1770 and 1806, 174 ships perished off the headland, and Trinity House was persuaded to erect a light on the Head in 1806. It was designed by Samuel Wyatt, consultant engineer to Trinity House, and built by the architect John Matson of Bridlington. The elegant, white tower houses only a staircase, the keeper's accommodation being clustered around the base.

A path leads south-west along the cliff top from the head, passing South Landing, Flamborough's ancient port, and Beacon Hill, probably the site of a Roman signal station, before reaching the ravine which marks the southern end of Danes Dyke. Sublime cliffs and romantic ravine all played their part in attracting eighteenth century visitors to Bridlington, now only a couple of miles distant.

But first a diversion, via a footpath which runs inland from the cliffs, to Sewerby House, overlooking the sea midway between ravine and town. The mansion occupies the site of a medieval manor house owned by the Sewerby family, then lords of the manor. John Greame built anew in 1714-20, and his three-storey, seven-bay block comprises the central section of the present Sewerby House. There were substantial alterations around 1807-8, including the addition of attractive bow-fronted wings, although these were only raised to their full height in 1848. Since 1931 the house and its park have been used by Bridlington Council as leisure facilities, the relaxed façade welcoming visitors to an unusual seaside site.

Stroll on into Bridlington. Intuitively, one heads for the harbour as the focus of all activity in a resort, but the town actually originated a mile inland, in the area now known as the Old Town, although the coastal settlement, the Quay, existed as early as 1100. Twelfth century Bridlington was a market town, based on High Street, which was probably extended north to form Market Place after the grant of a market and fair in 1200.

Port and town grew up together, with the coastal shipping trade complementing the inland market, until the mid-eighteenth century, when the arrival of visitors brought the resort of Bridlington into existence and tipped the developmental balance in favour of the sea front, where it has remained. The Quay became fashionable, while the arrival of the railway in 1846 brought mass tourism and concomitant building — hotels and entertainment venues in particular. Modern Bridlington concentrates more on conferences than circuses, but the resort, even without its lost people's palaces, is still attractive, and the harbour is a delight.

So to begin with, a look at Bridlington's beginning: the priory. It was an Augustinian

Edwardian holidaymakers on the North Pier at Bridlington, with the Floral Pavilion — built in 1904 and still in use — in the centre background.

foundation, established around 1115-20, but although monastic buildings seem to have been under construction during the twelfth century, little of significance remains from that period. The present church, St Mary the Virgin — normally known as the Priory Church — resulted from thirteenth century rebuilding on the site of the original priory church, which dated from Norman times. The new church was around 333 feet in length, but the whole structure east of the nave was demolished after the suppression of the priory in 1537, leaving just the 185 foot nave; today, its eastern bays function as a chancel. Inside, look to the south aisle for a black marble slab, possibly the tomb cover of Walter de Gant, founder of the priory. It dates from the twelfth century and its carved decoration combines architecture and strange beasts.

Of the monastic buildings, only the gate-house, known as the Bayle, survived the post-suppression destruction. It was probably built around 1388 and is a two-storey, brick and stone arched gateway. This near-total demo-

Fishing boats moored at Chicken Run Jetty in the centre of Bridlington harbour. The jetty was built in 1904; unfortunately, the origin of its name is unknown.

lition was a sad end for the priory, brought about by the participation of its last prior, William Wood, in the Pilgrimage of Grace. His punishment for this treasonable offence was execution, suppression of the priory, and the forfeit of its property to the Crown. It would have been particularly interesting to see the luxurious accommodation provided by the priory for the archbishops of York on their occasional visitations to the east, but it was not to be.

The buildings of High Street, in the Old Town to the west of the priory along Kirkgate, make a worthwhile detour before heading down to the sea front via St Johns Street and Quay Road. The shops and houses fronting on to narrow High Street are generally Georgian, although a little medieval stonework

Fishermen at the end of the North Pier, Bridlington. The navigation light marks the harbour entrance.

may be still found, and some smaller houses probably date from the seventeenth century. The bowed shop-fronts were added in a period of rebuilding during the late eighteenth century.

Even in 1821 the Quay was a substantial settlement, and by 1850 Quay and Old Town were linked by an almost-continuous built-up zone extending along Quay Road. Amenities available to early visitors included the Esplanade, a select walk running along the north cliff, and the Victoria Rooms, an assembly room-cum-ballroom.

Towards the end of the nineteenth century the resort became less of a fashionable haunt and more a destination for trippers; over 450 boarding houses were trading in the early 1890s. The demands of the mass market led to the construction of a series of entertainment buildings: the People's Palace, a concert hall and ballroom located near the east end of Quay Road, and the New Spa Theatre, the striking, creamy-white structure on South Marine Drive beside the harbour, were both erected in 1896. The Floral Pavilion, a miniature winter garden sited north of the harbour on Royal Princes Parade, was put up in 1904, while the Grand Pavilion was erected in 1906. Two of these, the New Spa and Grand Pavilion, were designed by Mangnall & Littlewoods, a Manchester architectural practice known for their seaside work, which included the wonderfully decorative Winter Gardens in Blackpool.

The busy harbour is now the resort's centre, and quite an entertainment in itself. In 1816, work began on enlarging the harbour and replacing the original timber and stone breakwaters by stone piers. It was 1843 before the 608 foot north pier was complete (it was extended by about 120 feet in 1866), while the south pier, around 1,500 feet long, was built in 1843-8. Chicken Run Jetty, in the centre of the harbour, was the site of the original south pier; it dates from 1904, but was rebuilt in 1950.

A bracing stroll to the beacon at end of the north pier makes a fitting finale to a day at the seaside, as enjoyable now as when the first day-trippers invaded the quiet resort in the 1870s. In Bridlington as in Filey, the traditional English seaside holiday is alive and well.

THE FINEST FORTIFICATION
Beverley and Hull

UNDOUBTEDLY THE most splendid approach to Beverley is by train from Hull, to the south: the Minster grows inexorably in size until it seems the carriages must career straight through its intricate stonework, only for the track to veer away eastward at the last moment. Passengers are deposited in the polite confines of Beverley Station, and the Minster is only a short walk back along Railway Street, across Wednesday Market and into Highgate.

Beverley itself is almost separate from the Minster, and lies to the north of the sumptuous and beautiful church, but the early history of town and Minster are closely bound together.

St John of Beverley, bishop of York in AD 705-18, is said to have founded a monastery in Beverley around AD 705, and been buried there in AD 721. Whatever the truth behind the legend, by the eleventh century it was widely regarded as accurate, and Beverley eventually became an important ecclesiastical centre on the strength of this tale. The original monastery was probably sacked by the Danes about AD 866, but a collegiate church, St John, was set up around AD 935 to serve the community.

Town and Minster then evolved together, although both were badly affected by fire in 1188. As the town became economically successful, its centre of gravity moved away from the Minster, with a series of new market places coming into existence between the twelfth and sixteenth centuries. The cloth industry prospered in medieval Beverley, when the town's population was probably around 5,000; it was twice the size of Hull in 1377. The suffix 'gate', which is attached to several Beverley street names, derives from the Norse word for street. The town may have been defended by a ditch in the thirteenth century, but there was never a wall; the remaining gateway, North Bar, was rebuilt in 1409-10.

The cloth industry declined in the post-medieval period, as did the town's function as a trading centre; the rise of West Riding textiles and the port of Hull were the respective

Beverley Minster from the south. Building the Minster took around 200 years, beginning in 1220.

reasons behind the changes. The sixteenth century was a particularly poor time for Beverley, but during the seventeenth and eighteenth centuries much rebuilding took place, as the town became a fashionable setting for the town houses of the country gentry of the East Riding. There were even a few ambitious private gardens, and several notable public buildings. Victorian Beverley saw a change of tone, when a working-class suburb expanded to the east, while the railway arrived in 1846 and industry — tanning, iron-founding and engineering — stimulated growth.

Any exploration of Beverley is incomplete without an excursion to the Minster, and if followed by a stroll through the centre to the excellent church of St Mary, will provide a comprehensive introduction to the architectural delights of the town.

And so, to the Minster. On the heels of the damaging fire in 1188 came another disaster, when the Minster tower fell in 1213. The present church postdates these misfortunes: the chancel and crossing were erected during 1220-70, beginning with the east end, while the nave dates from 1308-49; the west front, with its soaring twin towers, was added in 1390-1420. The stone is largely magnesian limestone from Tadcaster.Approaching the Minster along Highgate gives some idea of the medieval experience of the juxtaposition of church and town, as the towers rise above tight-knit, albeit mainly Georgian, houses; but the most picturesque view is from the south, where the cathedral-sized structure looms above a green meadow.

Once inside, there is much thirteenth-century blank arcading, with shafts of Purbeck marble, and an elegant double staircase in the north aisle of the chancel; this led to the octagonal chapter house, demolished in 1550. The Percy screen, behind the high altar, is a magnificently ornate stone screen dating from around 1334. It originally carried the shrine of St John of Beverley, whose tomb is marked by a slab at the east end of the nave. Just to the north of the high altar is the heavily-enriched Percy tomb, a monumentally splendid memorial to members of the Percy family, which dates from the mid-fourteenth century. Look, too, for memorials to the Warton family, sixteenth century Hull merchants who later became lords of the manor of Beverley.

There is much more: the choir stalls, dating from 1520, have a wonderful selection of misericords, sixty-eight in all, which are attributed to the Ripon school of wood-carvers. For highlights, choose from the ape on horseback, the sow and bagpipes, or the unicorn. Unseen above the crossing is a great survivor from the Minster's construction, the huge tread-wheel crane used for hauling masonry up into the tower. There has been much restoration at the Minster, and the list of architects involved over the years includes Nicholas Hawksmoor, who helped with repairs during 1717-30, and Sir George Gilbert Scott, responsible for the new choir screen and other works during 1863-80.

Altogether, the Minster offers a unique display of medieval and Georgian decorative carving, as well as a brief history of local politics, conveyed by means of monumental inscriptions.

Even after such an architectural feast, the buildings of Beverley itself are far from an anticlimax; indeed, the church of St Mary alone would be attraction enough for any other town. But before striking out towards the centre, there are two worthwhile detours to west and east of the Minster.

On Keldgate, which leads away from the south-west corner of the Minster, stands Anne Routh's Hospital, built in 1748-50. The impressive façade features a fine pediment above three large, blank arches; these almshouses are the work of James Moyser, amateur architect, friend of Lord Burlington and resident of Beverley, who was also partly responsible for the design of a few Yorkshire country houses, including Nostell Priory and Bretton Hall.

Architectural enthusiasts with time to spare might head along Flemingate, which runs south-east from the Minster, to reach Beckside. Here, a short terrace of mid to late Georgian houses stands beside Beverley Beck, a three-quarter mile stream which links the town with the River Hull to the east. As early as the thirteenth century, boats used the town's wharf at Grovehill — where the waters meet — and the beck, improved and kept in good repair, was important to the success of the town's industries. Unlike many larger canals and navigations, Beverley Beck has continued in constant use until the present day, although not as a commercial waterway.Bear right from Beckside into Hull Road, and right again into Figham Road to find the gasworks, where a Classical gateway (using the Tuscan order) marks out the gasworks. It dates from 1824 and the coming of a public gas supply to Beverley. Initially, only the streets were lit by gas, but by the late 1820s there were also nearly 100 private consumers.

Now back to the Minster and into the town proper. Good Georgian houses are all around, with an enjoyable variety of doorcases and fanlights, although their most decorative elements — plasterwork and staircases — are largely invisible to the passer-by. From Wednesday Market, follow Butcher Row until it bends left into Toll Gavel. Here, a diversion down Cross Street into Register Square is in order, and a confrontation with the massive Greek Doric portico of the guildhall, a medieval building reconstructed in 1762-5 by William Middleton, the leading local builder of the time. The superb interior has plasterwork by Giuseppe Cortese of York. However, on a flying visit, it is the portico which takes the eye. It was added in 1832, and is by Charles Mountain of Hull, a local specialist in the Greek Revival style.

Return to Toll Gavel, turning left to pass the strange shop front of number forty-four, where a pair of snakes slither upwards, entwined around the columns of the porch. This peculiarity, which marks a former chemists

shop, dates from around 1830; the snakes symbolise Aesculapius, the Roman god of medicine.

On to the centrepiece of Beverley, Saturday Market. The market cross is a happily bumptious affair, an octagonal canopy supported by eight Tuscan columns, topped by a mildly Baroque roof dotted with urns. It was erected in 1711-14 by local landowners Sir Michael Warton and Sir Charles Hotham, and was designed by Theophilus Shelton of Wakefield; Shelton, actually a lawyer, had already worked in Beverley, building a school on Highgate in 1710. At the northern end of the main market place is the red-brick corn exchange, built in 1886 in Baroque style. From 1910 it has functioned as a cinema, the Picture Playhouse, and although other uses have intervened, the delightful interior has changed only a little.

Just past the northern end of Saturday Market, at the start of North Bar Within, is the church of St Mary. This intriguing building is the antidote to the cool lines of the Minster, for those who need a further helping of beastly misericords, or a sight of Beverley's five generous 'minstrels'. There was a Norman church on this site, but most of the present structure dates from the thirteenth century onwards. Its central tower collapsed in 1520, crashing through nave and transepts, although the west front, dating from about 1400, remained intact. The tower and nave (inside the aisles) were rebuilt in the following decade.

Once inside, inspect the nave piers for the names of those who contributed to their rebuilding after 1520; the 'wyffes' or wives of Beverley were donors, as were the 'maynstrells' or minstrels. Five of the latter appear

The New Walk, Beverley, in the peaceful era around the turn of the century when traffic was horse-drawn.

in person, as it were, in a happy group clinging to the easternmost pillar of the north arcade. The wooden panels of the chancel roof are decorated with paintings of forty English kings, concluding with Henry VI. The original work was carried out in 1445, but it was overpainted in 1863 and again in 1939; however, it still looks splendid, and gives a reasonable impression of the fifteenth-century chancel. Below the kings are the choir stalls, dating from around 1425-50, with twenty-three fine misericords. Here, amongst others, we find ape as doctor (on the north side) and elephant and castle (south).

From St Mary, turn north along North Bar Within to pass through the brick archway of the North Bar, which dates from 1409-10. It is no surprise to find that the street beyond the bar is North Bar Without, and is pleasantly open after the constrictions of the town within. In medieval times, those wishing to enter the town gathered in the area beyond the bar, which also served as a market place for animals. From the seventeenth century the gen-

THE FINEST FORTIFICATION   105

try began to build along North Bar Without, and its ornamental extension, New Walk, was laid out in 1782. Of the excellent houses on North Bar Without, look particularly at number fifty-six (on the north side); its Rococo doorcase dates from 1765.

Return through the bar and turn left at St Mary, to head out of town along Norwood, which becomes Hull Bridge Road (A1035). At the junction with the A1174, turn south for Hull. To the east of the road lies Swinemoor, one of Beverley's three remaining medieval common pastures. With Figham, to the southeast, and Westwood, to the west of town (there are fine views of the Minster from the A1079 and B1230 as they cross this common), the pasture-land totals some 1,200 acres. Swinemoor itself may date from the thirteenth century; a massive bank and ditch, created to keep animals from straying, still survives.

Running south across Swinemoor is the impressively lengthy Beverley and Barmston Drain; as its name suggests, the drain played a vital part in draining the valley west of the River Hull, after the passing of its eponymous act of parliament in 1798. It runs for fifteen miles in huge, straight stretches beside the River Hull from Hempholme, about six miles north of Beverley, to meet the river in Hull itself. The A1174 veers around the eastern outskirts of Beverley, crosses Beverley Beck, then Beverley Drain, before joining the A1079 to hurtle into Hull. If there is time for a more measured approach, turn west off the trunk road on the B1233 for Cottingham and a circuitous route to the city, taking in the estimable Humber Bridge.

Cottingham, now part of Hull's ever-growing suburbs, is an ancient village; it had a medieval castle, probably built in the thirteenth century but gone by the sixteenth century, while its church, St Mary, is a large, fourteenth to fifteenth century edifice. Much of the Victorian stained glass in St Mary was produced in Belgium, to the designs of John Capronnier; his work was popular in Yorkshire, but its brightness always comes as a shock in the typically muted English country church.

The site of Baynard Castle, Cottingham's own, is just east of the B1233 (West End Road) as it approaches the Lawns, Hull University's halls of residence. The remains of mound and moat are visible behind the houses. The castle, originally a fortified manor house, was strengthened and crenellated after 1327, and the area was still prosperous in the early fifteenth century. Decline seems to have set in later in the century, probably due to worsening of the climate and disease.

To leave Cottingham, take the B1233 northwest to its meeting with the A164, then join the new road to head south, passing the wooded grounds of Castle Hill Hospital in a mile or so. Within the woods and fairly close to the road is a white, hexagonal tower, a Gothic eyecatcher for Cottingham Castle, itself put up in 1814-15 but demolished following a fire.

Now south through Willerby to Kirk Ella, where the church of St Andrew, in Church Lane, harbours a worthwhile set of monuments. In particular, Joseph Sykes — Hull merchant and twice mayor of the city — escapes from his coffin, only to find himself involved in a busy scene with trumpet-blowing angel, galleon, assorted symbolic ladies and a few rocks for good measure. The gentleman died in 1805 and his memorial, the work of John Bacon, dates from 1809.

Wealthier Hull merchants began to move out of the city from the late eighteenth century, inducing a competition for suitable country houses. The Sykes made their family home at West Ella Hall, about a mile west of Kirk Ella, and went on to enlarge West Ella village in the mid-nineteenth century by building some prettily-bargeboarded houses in the main street.

Turn south off the A164 at Anlaby, taking the B1232 for Hessle, the Humber Estuary and the mighty bridge. The village of Hessle, with its medieval church and some very decent Georgian dwellings, is interesting for its own sake, but proximity to Hull and the coming of the crossing have ensured that the settlement is best known for being left behind: by travellers to the city, across the bridge and even along the Wolds Way. The footpath starts at Hessle Haven, about half a mile east of the bridge, and gives a splendid view of the structure, under which it passes (alternatively, there is a special viewing area near the bridge).

The Humber Bridge, opened on the 17th July 1981, is currently the longest single-span suspension bridge in the world. The length of the span between the reinforced concrete towers is 1,480 yards, the total cost was £91 million and building took over eight years; the engineers were Freeman, Fox & Partners. The north bank tower, which overshadows the footpath in every way, is 509 feet high, and the road deck is suspended nearly 100 feet above the water at high tide. Approaching by road, the bridge is best seen from the south bank on the descent from the Lincolnshire Wolds, but the walk beneath the stupendous superstructure on the north bank is not to be missed. It is unnerving and awesome to be so close to an epic feat of engineering, and the huge scale is often lost on those who simply cross by car.

From Hessle, road and railway lead inexorably to Kingston-upon-Hull, almost invariably known as Hull. The city began life as the medieval new town of Wyke-upon- Hull which, even then, was often simply called Hull. Its site was the point at which the River Hull met the Humber Estuary (near the present High Street), and it was founded in the late twelfth century by the Cistercian abbey of Meaux, three miles east of Beverley, to provide an outlet for their wool production.

In 1293 Edward I bought the town from the abbey — renaming it Kingston-upon-Hull — as a base for his Scottish campaigning; it then comprised around sixty houses and seventy unbuilt plots, arranged on a rough grid plan. After Edward's intervention the town expanded rapidly, becoming a borough in 1299 and acquiring extra markets and fairs.

In 1321-4 Edward II built the defensive fortifications, comprising earthen ramparts, palisade and ditch, which were to act as a boundary and a limit to the town's growth until the late eighteenth century. These defences were rebuilt in brick between the late 1330s and 1410. The fourteenth century port of Hull was prosperous; trade with the Baltic states was particularly important, and the warehouses and houses of merchants filled the area between High Street and the River Hull.

The following century saw a slight decline, but the visit of Henry VIII to Hull in 1541 resulted in his decision to construct a castle,

An Edwardian afternoon on busy George Street in central Hull. At this time the site of Queen's Gardens, which lies just to the south, was still functioning as a dock; it was infilled during the 1930s.

blockhouses (fortified firing positions) and new walls to defend the eastern boundary, all of which gave a fillip to the town. The defences were again strengthened during the Civil War, and in the 1680s the castle and south blockhouse were incorporated into a daunting, moated citadel. By this time, symbolism was more to the point than the reality of defence. Celia Fiennes visited Hull in 1697 and was impressed by the martial display, remarking

that 'were it finished is thought it would be the finest fortification that could be seen'.

Finished it never was, and the walls increasingly became a constraint upon Hull's growth. Congestion in the old harbour resulted in the digging of an artificial dock — called the Dock — on the site of the northern defences in 1774-8. A Georgian new town arose north of the Dock, and the western defences were pulled down by the end of the century. The second dock, New Dock, was built in 1803-9, and several more followed. The railway arrived in 1840, and prosperity, based on shipping, fishing and allied port industries, lasted throughout the Victorian era — Hull becoming a city in 1897 — and into the Edwardian period.

However, decline during the 1930s was followed by disaster in 1940 when the first German bomber raid struck, and by the end of the war many of the city's warehouses and much of its housing had been destroyed. Despite these losses, and some over-enthusiastic rebuilding during the postwar years, there is much to be seen in Hull, much that is both memorable and unusual.

Make a start at Hull Paragon, an apt name for this most excellent railway station. When the railway arrived in Hull from Selby in 1840, its terminus was Kingston Street, at the logical end of its route along the Humber Estuary. After the Bridlington service began in 1846, a more central terminus became necessary, and so G T Andrews of the York & North Midland Railway designed Paragon (unromantically named after Paragon Street, rather than for its fine qualities), which opened in 1848. His Italianate building forms the south side of the present station, while his trainshed, which originally covered nine platforms, is happily intact.

Inside the terminus is a wooden, Art Nouveau kiosk, originally used as a refreshment room; it is this esoteric touch which

Tiles in the old booking office of Hull Paragon station; the trainshed can be glimpsed through the window. The colourful booking office was an Edwardian addition to the station.

alerts the unwary passenger to the nature of the unique booking hall beyond. Cream, green and brown tiles are all around this lofty space, which centres on a magnificent former booking office of carved oak. Clocks surmount the corners, while its twelve windows allowed Edwardian clerks to issue tickets for the destinations once listed on panels above, which included such enticing notions as '1,000-mile tickets' and 'Pleasure Parties'. The hall, now somewhat neglected, was a product of alterations made to the station by North Eastern Railway architect William Bell in 1904-5; its mosaic floor displays the NER motif.

The Edwardian traveller would have emerged into the city through a massive iron *porte cochere*—also part of the Bell reconstruction—but as with London's celebrated Euston Arch, this was demolished, making way for a tedious office block in 1962. However, the Royal Station Hotel has survived to remind passengers of the railway age. It was built in 1851 by Andrews in Italianate style, and extended twice, by Bell at the time of the other alterations, and again in 1935. Following a fire in 1990 the hotel, now known simply as the Royal Hotel, has been completely restored.

Before crossing to Paragon Street, opposite the station, look to the right, around the corner into Anlaby Road. The Tower Cinema, with its ceramic façade and two golden domes — actually covered in glass mosaic — was designed in 1914 by Horace Percival Binks. He topped this pleasant, Art Nouveau work with an allegorical lady holding a camera and roll of film.

Close by is the College of Art, built in 1904, an exuberant piece of Edwardian Baroque by the London practice of Lanchester, Stewart and Rickards, specialists in public buildings. The brilliant design skills of Edwin Rickards provided the impetus for their success in architectural competitions. At the College of Art, Rickards broke up the main façade with an oriel window, and decorated the pedimented gable with a pictorial tile-panel.

Now into Paragon Street, which ends at Hull's premier public space, Queen Victoria Square. Its character has changed greatly since the dock to the north-east of the square was filled in during the inter-war years. This was the city's first dock, initially called the Dock or Old Dock when built in 1774-8, then renamed Queen's Dock in 1854. With ten acres of water, it was at one time the largest dock in England, but by 1930 it had come to be seen as a barrier between old Hull and new development in the west of the city, and after infilling was replaced by Queen's Gardens.

Amazingly, the process has continued during the late twentieth century, as Prince's Dock (built as Junction Dock in 1826-9), to the south of the present square, has partially disappeared under the Prince's Quay shopping centre. The façade of the new glass emporium is only moderately interesting, and once inside, there is barely a glimpse of water. Was this the best solution for what could have been the city's greatest asset — water as an integral part of its being? The intimate relationship between docks and shops created a distinctive image which set Hull apart from other cities, but now there is just another shopping centre, a high street in a box.

The triple-domed Dock Offices of 1867-71 is the most imposing building on Queen Victoria Square; now cut off from the remaining docks, it provides a necessary

This ceramic lady (reputed to be Mary Pickford) complete with her camera and film, sits decoratively above the Tower Cinema in Hull.

The ceramic façade of the Tower Cinema, Hull, built in 1914. The clean-cut but Classical appearance of the cinema was designed to present a combination of modernity, respectability and excitement to prospective patrons.

reminder of the significance of shipping and trade to the city's history. Although the triangular edifice has an unforgettable silhouette, in truth its vaguely Renaissance styling, by Christopher George Wray — a little-known London architect who won the job in competition — is bland. However, the domes are a triumph.

The city hall, designed by Hull's first city architect, Joseph H Hirst, in 1903-9, sits across the square from the Dock Offices (which is now a museum). It is a suitably powerful Edwardian Baroque work, complete with dome. The city hall followed on from the town hall, built by Hull's own Cuthbert Brodrick, architect of the magnificent Leeds

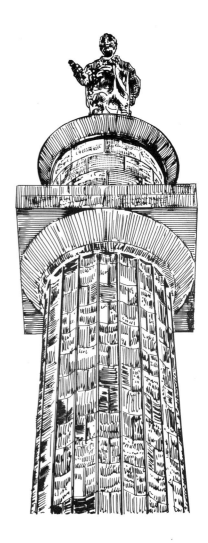

The Wilberforce Column, Hull, reflected in a Queen's Gardens pond. The gardens were created by the infilling of Queen's Dock during the 1930s.

The ninety-foot Wilberforce Column was put up in 1834 to commemorate William Wilberforce, local man and anti-slave trade campaigner.

town hall, in 1862. His Italianate pile was demolished to make way for the guildhall in 1906-14; Hull's urge to renew has certainly had some notable casualties.

Near the city hall, on the corner of Carr Lane, is the cheerful Punch Hotel of 1896, red brick with an Elizabethan-cum-Gothic façade in buff Burmantofts terracotta. It was the work of Smith, Brodrick & Lowther, the local practice which carried on after Cuthbert Brodrick left the profession, and the country, in 1869; he had recently been placed second in the Hull Dock Offices competition.

Before leaving the square and heading eastward to the River Hull, a visit to Queen's Gardens is essential. At the far end is the ninety-foot Wilberforce Column, erected in 1834 (on a nearby site) to commemorate William Wilberforce, emancipator of slaves and son of Hull, who died in the previous year. Public subscriptions provided the funds for the Doric column, which was designed by John Clark of Leeds in his favourite Greek Revival style, then popular in Hull.

Dominating the skyline to the south of the gardens are two huge sculptures, which crown the guildhall on Alfred Gelder Street. The building was designed by Sir Edwin Cooper, but 'Maritime Prowess' and 'Strength' were by Albert Hodge, who also worked on the façade of the Victoria and Albert Museum.

Take Whitefriargate, at the south-east corner of Queen Victoria Square, to pass that memorably-named alley, Land of Green Ginger — possibly named after the site of the warehouses in which imported ginger was stored — and reach the junction with Silver Street.

Trinity House Lane, the home of **Trinity House**, is to the right. Trinity House **of Hull** originated with a religious guild founded **in** 1369, but by the mid-fifteenth century it **had** become the guild of the mariners, concerned with the well-being of its members and their families. Later it became involved with shipping control and the provision of lighthouses; these latter functions were taken over by Trinity House of Deptford in 1836. The main Trinity House building on this complex site dates from 1753-9, and has a fine carved pediment, including figures of Neptune and Britannia, above a nine-bay façade; the sculptor was local craftsman Jeremiah Hargrave, but the standard of his work was as high as any in the country. Trinity House, with its heavily-decorated court room, epitomises the best of Hull's Georgian building boom, which was linked to the port's growing prosperity.

Turn back into Silver Street, where Ye Olde White Harte awaits. Inside the pub is a finely-panelled first floor parlour, and a fireplace ornamented by a collection of nineteenth-century Dutch tiles, their blue designs on a white base including an assortment of biblical scenes.

These few, but excellent, tiles will serve as an introduction to the ceramic delights of Hull's pubs — glistening façades, curving bar counters — which are scattered about the city, but well worth pursuing. The terracotta of the Punch Hotel in Queen Victoria Square is unusual in this context, as most of Hull's decorative Victorian and Edwardian pubs use glazed ceramics to make their point — which was, of course, to advertise their wares and entice the prospective customer into colourful surroundings quite unlike home.

Prince's Quay shopping centre rising above the waters of Prince's Dock, Hull. The dock, the city's third, was built as Junction Dock in 1826-9, and renamed in 1854 in honour of Prince Albert.

The Dock Offices, Hull, built in 1867-71. The design of the triple-domed building resulted from an architectural competition, and its construction cost nearly £90,000.

In Alfred Gelder Street, just north of Silver Street (along Manor Street) is the White Hart, built around 1904 in blatant mock-Tudor style, complete with half-timbering and a balcony. Inside is a semicircular bar counter manufactured by Doulton, using green and yellow Art Nouveau faience. This is a truly sensuous piece, the complex curves of its cross-section harmonising with the grand sweep of the whole. Before 1981, the back bar was full of Minton ware, a bar counter and wall tiles, but it all became a prey to contemporary fashions in pub refurbishment, and was destroyed.

To journey further afield for a moment, Hessle Road (A1105) provides two excellent ceramic pubs: the Alexandra Hotel, near the city centre, and the Dairycoates Inn, about a mile out. The Alexandra has a most unusual exterior, combining shiny, brown and yellow faience in Edwardian Baroque forms with curves and even star-shapes made by its glazing bars. The façade of the Dairycoates is less flamboyant, apart from the elegant green, buff and white tiled panel featuring an an-chor and advertisng the pub's original owners, the Anchor Brewery. The brewery, in Silvester Street, just north of Queen's Gardens, was the home of the Hull Brewery Company, which ceased brewing in 1985.

Just over half a mile along Spring Bank

Springhead water-pumping station, Hull, in 1930; the towered, central building dates from 1862-4. The station was coal-fired until 1957, when it was converted to electricity. The supervisor's house, on the left, was occupied until this change took place.

(west from Beverley Road, the A1079), at the junction with Derringham Street is the Polar Bear. Anchors are displayed on the external stonework of this impressive corner pub, while inside is another semicircular bar counter, this time in shades of buff and brown. A worthwhile diversion from the Polar Bear lies three miles away off Spring Bank West, in Springhead Avenue. This is the Springhead water-pumping station, built in Italianate style by Thomas Dale in 1862-4. The steam-powered beam engine, which dates from 1876, is

supported by Doric columns; this architectural conceit reflects the significance with which the Victorians viewed the production of clean water. The pumping station is still operational, although now partly used as a museum.

Returning to central Hull and Silver Street, the route east continues across Lowgate and into Scale Lane. The buildings which catered for the needs of commerce in Victorian Hull cluster together in Lowgate, and display the high quality of work produced by local architects: the former Midland Bank (1869-70) and

Barges on the River Hull, near its meeting with the Humber Estuary on the southern edge of Hull. The river was still a busy waterway soon after the Second World War, when this photograph was taken.

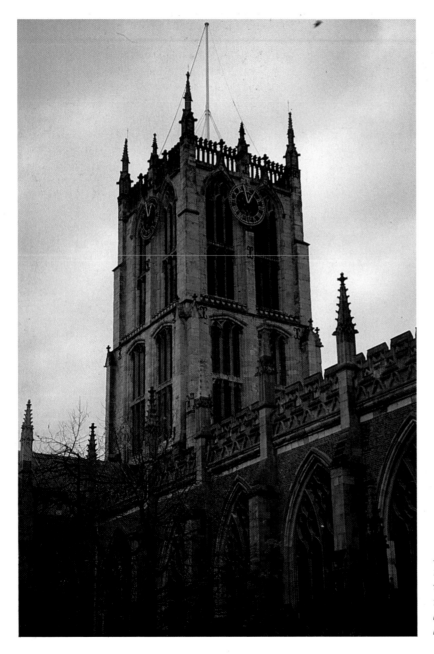

Holy Trinity Church, Hull. It is the third church on this site, which adjoins the city's open market, and building took around 200 years, beginning about 1300.

A fine ceramic panel — possibly Edwardian — on the façade of the Dairycoates Inn, Hessle Road, Hull. It advertises beer from the Anchor Brewery, home of the Hull Brewery Company.

Warehouses beside the River Hull, just south of Drypool Bridge. The warehouses back on to High Street, which was always the centre of the merchants' quarter in the port.

Hull Exchange Company offices (1865-6), both by William Botterill; and the Brodrick practice's Ocean Chambers (1899-1900). At the end of Scale Lane is High Street, which backs on to the River Hull, and from the early days of the port's existence was the merchants' quarter. Behind the houses on the east of the street lay gardens and private wharfs. High Street remained the city's most prestigious address until late in the eighteenth century.

In this street of notable buildings, look first for Wilberforce House, the home of William Wilberforce, built around 1660 but remodelled, by Wilberforce's father, in the mid-eighteenth century. His alterations left the interior with exquisite Rococo plasterwork. Further south and across the street is Maister House, rebuilt after a fire in 1743 by the leading merchant Henry Maister. Inside is a tremendous Palladian staircase designed by Joseph Page, Hull architect and master builder, with a complex and elegant ironwork balustrade by Robert Bakewell of Derby; the balustrade was shipped to Hull via the Trent.

The house of wealthy merchant and banker Joseph Pease at 18 High Street has been demolished, but his huge warehouses, built in 1745 and 1760 on the waterfront, still give an idea of the appearance of the river frontage during the late eighteenth century, when the wharf was lined with similar buildings. The regularly-spaced windows of the warehouses provided light and ventilation, while their small size indicates the limited load-bearing capacity of the major building material, brick. Later, the greater innate strength of iron-framed construction — the frame is hidden behind the brick façade — meant that windows could be larger.

Looking south along Hull's riverside walk to the tidal surge barrier at the mouth of the River Hull. The barrier, which protects the city from flooding, was completed in 1980.

The waterfront walk provides an excellent view of the warehouses to north and south, and of the tidal surge barrier at the mouth of the Hull. The monumental barrier is formed by a great bar, suspended between two

Holy Trinity Church, Hull, reflected in office windows across Market Place. Inside the church, on the south aisle of the nave, are two stained glass windows, designed in Arts and Crafts style by Walter Crane.

columns, which turns and descends to block the river in case of potential flooding. It was erected by the Yorkshire Water Authority and opened in 1980.

Turn back from the river, and head west along Church Lane to Market Place, where there is much of interest apart from the massive form of Holy Trinity Church, in area the largest parish church in England. On North Church Side is the tall tower of the Market Hall, built in 1902-4 by J H Hirst, while facing the west front of the church on South Church Side is the brick-built old grammar school, erected in 1583-5 and now a museum. A real surprise — but for gentlemen only — may be found underneath the statue of King William III (by Peter Scheemakers, and dating from 1734) just south-east of the church. Descend below the legs of the horse which carries the king, to find a superb gentlemen's toilets; terracotta from Ruabon and glorious tilework make a visit to this glamorous Edwardian loo a memorable occasion.

Back up the steps to see Holy Trinity towering 150 feet above; its sheer size — the length is 285 feet — and the early use of brick in its construction make Holy Trinity a rarity amongst churches. It was established about 1285 and the present structure, the third on the site, was the first major English church to use brick as the main building material. The transepts were begun around 1300, followed by the chancel during the mid-fourteenth century, the nave in 1389-1418 and the tower about 1500.

The first impression of the interior is one of brightness, with many clear windows illuminating the vast space of the nave. Look out for monuments to various members of the Maister family, and, in the south aisle of the choir, an alabaster effigy of Sir William de la Pole, who died in 1366. He was the richest commoner in England, a Hull trader in wine, corn and especially wool, who became the town's first mayor and eventually did service for the king.

But do not miss a pair of stained glass windows in the south aisle of the nave, opposite the pulpit. They were produced by the combined talents of two artists and designers: Walter Crane, stalwart of the Arts and Crafts movement, and his younger collaborator, J Silvester Sparrow.

Crane began his career as a painter, but eventually turned his hand to a great range of practical design tasks, and founded the Northern Art Workers' Guild in 1896. Of Crane and Sparrow's work at Holy Trinity, the brighter Earle window, a representation of psalm 148, *O Praise the Lord of Heaven*, is stylistically influenced by William Morris and dates from 1897. The Brooks window of 1907 shows the brooding form of the crucifixion in rich, dark hues. Colourful, unusual and idiosyncratic, the pair of windows suit church and city to perfection.

NOTHING REMARKABLE?

Holderness

THE HUMMOCKY plain of Holderness, east of the Wolds and on the road to nowhere, has not always proved attractive to travellers. Glacial and post-glacial deposits formed its gently undulating countryside, bounded by clay cliffs generally reaching only about thirty feet in height, and now subject to fearsome erosion. Yorkshire's losing battle with the sea has its outcome at Spurn Head, that unstable peninsula fuelled with sand and shingle dragged south by the waves.

Holderness can indeed be bleak, but it is far from unrewarding. Its builders and architects have left us some enjoyable peculiarities, and it is impossible to agree with that prolific writer Daniel Defoe, who gave his verdict on a visit to the Holderness coast during the early 1720s: 'the most that I find remarkable here is that there is nothing remarkable'.

Let us begin at Wansford, three miles southeast of Great Driffield, on the edge of the plain where the Wolds merge slowly into Holderness. Wansford stands just north of the River Hull and the canalised section of the Driffield Navigation; a carpet mill was built between the two around 1790, but had ceased to function by the mid-nineteenth century, and has now vanished, leaving some workers' cottages nearby.

A chapel existed in the village prior to 1330, while the manor passed to Sir Christopher Sykes of Sledmere in 1787. The church of St Mary was built for the second Sir Tatton Sykes by his favourite architect, G E Street, in 1866-8. It has a prettily-painted chancel roof, and a splendid Gothic screen of marble, alabaster and iron; this probably dates from the 1870s. Street also designed the parsonage and school for the little estate village, which was sold by the Sykes family in 1920.

Before heading south into Holderness proper, let us cross the bridge at Wansford to explore the area west of the River Hull; a by-road through Skerne leads eventually to Hutton Cranswick, just off the A164. The settlement is actually a pair of villages: Hutton to the north, set out around a triangular green by the church of St Peter; and Cranswick to the south, a rambling collection of houses with a larger green.

Take the by-road leading west from Cranswick, which edges up into the Wolds on a roundabout route to Kilnwick. Kilnwick Hall, home of the Grimston family, was demolished in 1951, but the massive wall of the kitchen garden remains from the mid-eighteenth century, and assorted Grimston monuments may be found in All Saints Church, restored in 1871.

A mile or so south is Lockington, where the church of St Mary has painted panelling dating from the seventeenth century on show in its Estoft chapel. The church itself has a Norman south doorway, thirteenth century nave and tower, and mainly fourteenth century chancel. The south chapel was reconstructed as the Estoft family chapel in 1634-5, and its wood panelling was painted with a total of 173 shields, all having some connection with the family. This oddity was restored in 1851.

A mile east of Lockington is the A164, with Scorborough a mile to the south. Scorborough village church, St Leonard, was provided by James Hall of Scorborough Hall; Hall was agent to the Hotham family of Dalton Hall, three miles to the west. St Leonard was built in 1857-9 by John Loughborough Pearson, and clearly the funds made available to him were more than ample. A couple of miles further south is Leconfield, where the Percy family built a manor house, crenellated after 1308; there was also a large deer park.

The route east is blocked by the River Hull, so return up the A164 to Watton. The church of St Mary, off the main road, is peculiar: brick-built, in a late sixteenth or early seventeenth century version of Gothic. Just as interesting is Watton Priory, close to the church. It was founded as a Gilbertine house — England's only home-grown order — around 1150; being a nunnery served by canons, two separate sets of accommodation were required. The nuns lived in the west of the double house, and the canons in the east; the surviving prior's house dates from the fourteenth century. More impressive is the fifteenth-century prior's hall, with a wonderfully delicate two-storey, pentagonal bow-window topped by a pyramidal roof.

But now for the plain of Holderness; head back across the River Hull at Wansford, then turn south on the B1249 for Frodingham Bridge and the coast at Skipsea.

Just before the village, which is about a mile from the sea, look north over the meadows to see a great mound, nearly fifty feet high; this is all that remains of Skipsea Castle, once home to Drogo de la Beuvriere, the first lord of Holderness. William the Conquerer granted Holderness — then almost an island — to the Flemish soldier Drogo soon after 1071. Drogo was married to a relative of William, and legend tells us that Drogo accidentally killed his wife and rushed home to Flanders, never to return. It is, however, certain that William took back Holderness in 1087, then gave it to the counts of Aumale from Normandy, who were lords of Holderness until the failure of their line in the 1270s.

Drogo built Skipsea Castle, at what is known today as Skipsea Brough, in the latter part of the eleventh century. The castle, on top of its motte or mound, was connected to the bailey by a causeway which spanned one of the many Holderness meres; apart from Hornsea Mere, the largest lake in the East

On the left is the mound of eleventh-century Skipsea Castle. The tower of All Saints Church, Skipsea, can be seen in the distance, across the site of the old mere.

Riding, all these meres have long since been drained to reclaim the land for agricultural use.

Drogo's castle survived his flight, but its position in the north of Holderness meant that it was ill-suited as an administrative centre, and the counts of Aumale made their headquarters at Burstwick, three miles east of Hedon. By about 1200, Skipsea Castle had been abandoned, and its destruction was ordered in 1221 by the king, as retribution for a local rebellion. To climb the motte, take the footpath which leads north from the road at Skipsea Brough. Although the castle has disappeared, perhaps the view, which takes in Flamborough as well as medieval All Saints Church at Skipsea, has not changed too much since Drogo's days of power. Turn south from Skipsea, taking the by-road which runs south-east from Skipsea Brough to Bewholme. In this little hamlet, on Far Lane, stands a fine row of cottages constructed from cobble. This peculiarly local building material — mainly stones retrieved from the beaches of Holder-ness — has been used for churches, cottages and walls throughout the area, and lends a unique character to its villages.

The by-road west of Bewholme joins the A165 near the village of Brandesburton and its huge Victorian hall, now a hospital. The church of St Mary in Brandesburton — also a cobble building apart from its brick clerestory and porch — is home to a pair of interesting brasses, both featuring dogs. Sir John de St Quintin, who died in 1397, is shown with a greyhound beneath his feet, while his wife Lora is accompanied by a little dog with bells on its collar.

Continue south along the A165 to Leven, two miles distant. The village stands just over three miles east of the River Hull, to which it is connected by the Leven Canal, built for about £6,000 at the expense of the Bethells, landowners from nearby Rise Park, and opened around 1804.

The Bethells had been involved with the passage of the Beverley and Barmston Drain-age Act in 1798, and were keen agricultural improvers; apart from general trade with Hull, their canal was intended to carry lime and manure for agricultural use. The enterprise was a reasonable success, but eventually suf-fered in competition with the railways, and then road traffic. The Bethells closed the canal in 1935, and most of the warehouses at Leven Canal Head have been demolished, although a few remnants of its working life still remain.

A mile south of Leven is the junction with the A1035, marked by a Gothick house known as White Cross Cottage, which was built around 1761 as a toll house to mark the east end of the then new turnpike road between Leven and Beverley. Battlements, ogee-headed windows and a pristine, white façade make this a memorable landmark.

Head west on the A1035, then take the by-road leading south from Routh across the flat, wet fields of Routh Carrs. It is only a couple of miles to the site of Meaux Abbey, a Cistercian house founded in 1151.

The Cistercian order came to dominate the religious life of Holderness, and Meaux Ab-bey was prominent in colonising the plain, improving agricultural practices, and was also an important producer of tiles. Meaux was a wealthy house, with extensive thir-teenth and fourteenth century buildings, in-cluding church and cloisters, but the Black Death took forty out of its fifty monks and lay brothers in 1349, and dissolution finished off the process of decline. Only earthworks now survive as a reminder of its former status.

South of the abbey site, turn left at the bridge across Holderness Drain, and take the narrow lane towards South Skirlaugh, on the A165. The church of St Augustine, all pinna-cles and battlements, was built in 1401, and is thus totally Perpendicular in style; it was given by Bishop Skirlaw of Durham to his native village.

Head north on the B1243, through Rise, where Rise Park, home of the Bethell family, lies east of the main road. The mansion, built in 1815-20 for Richard Bethell, has a giant Ionic portico at the centre of its west façade.

The architects were probably Charles Watson and James Pigott Pritchett the elder of York.

At Sigglesthorne, turn east on to the B1244; in a mile or so, look out for Mushroom Cottage, built during 1812-14 in conjunction with Wassand Hall, just to the south. Country-house designer Thomas Cundy senior was responsible for both works. The cottage, which originally had a thatched roof, is a Picturesque, circular dwelling in rustic Gothick style. It is a happy product of the late eighteenth and early nineteenth century fashion for the overly ornamental, which was applied especially to estate and garden buildings. In contrast, Wassand Hall is a fairly plain villa.

Hornsea ia a couple of miles further east, beside its 467 acre mere. Medieval Hornsea lay along a single street by the eastern edge of the mere, with the hamlet of Hornsea Beck a mile away on the coast. The hamlet was eventually washed away, and Hornsea itself expanded hardly at all until the first stirrings of interest in the village as a resort in the early nineteenth century; the end result was that the village grew to occupy the whole area between cliffs and mere.

Hornsea could boast bathing machines in 1809, and had come to the notice of the fashionable by 1822, but only in the 1830s were any buildings specifically constructed for the holiday trade. By the middle of the century the Marine Hotel and a few lodging houses were catering for a steady flow of visitors from Hull, and the arrival of the railway in 1864 ushered in the trippers. Hornsea never succeeded as a mass resort, however, and was perhaps more important as a commuter village for Hull (despite the closure of the railway), at least until the present day; now Hornsea Pottery, a huge shopping-cum-theme park, attracts the crowds which the resort itself failed to please.

Architecturally, Hornsea is a touch anonymous, with little flavour of the archetypal seaside resort. Its most imposing structure — despite the loss of its spire, which fell from the tower in 1733 — is the medieval church of St Nicholas. But a nice peculiarity may be found near the centre, off Newbegin. Bettison's Folly is a fifty foot high, brick-built tower of circular cross-section; it was erected by the eponymous gentleman, who lived in nearby Tower House, in 1844. Its apparent purpose was to allow a servant early sight of his master returning from work, down Southorpe Hill from Hull, thus enabling dinner to be prepared at the correct moment. Perhaps. Tower House was demolished in 1966, but the folly, with its decorative pattern of projecting brick headers (short ends), remains intact.

Leave Hornsea to cruise down the coast on the B1242, through Mappleton and Aldbrough, bearing left after Garton and down to the seaside at Grimston. Here the delightful Grimston Garth hides in tree-decked parkland close to the water, an unusual setting for a distinctly peculiar house. It was built around 1781-7 for the landowner Thomas Grimston from Kilnwick, north of Beverley, by John Carr.

Triangular buildings were high fashion at that time, and although Carr worked his conservative way with the design, the house is still an oddity. At its centre is a two-storey castellated triangular block, which supports a further hexagonal storey, while a round tower projects from each corner of the main

Looking north along the promenade at Hornsea during the Edwardian era.

triangle. In the hexagon is a Gothick room, which was originally partnered by a Chinese room, since altered. A massive, turreted gatehouse, complete with portcullis, was added in the park around 1812, when the Gothic gatehouse had itself become a fashionable architectural item. Had Defoe been able to see Grimston Garth, he would undoubtedly have considered it remarkable.

A mile directly south of Grimston, just off the by-road to Hilston, is another strange structure, but here function rather than fashion is the explanation for its existence. Admiral Storr's Tower, an octagonal, brick building, was erected in 1750 to act as a seamark — a landmark for sailors. Now head west from Grimston, taking the by-road which leaves the B1242 at Garton, and pass through Humbleton to meet the B1238 a mile or so west of the splendid Burton Constable, one of Yorkshire's finest houses.

Burton Constable began life as a medieval pele tower, which was much enlarged about 1570 and further altered in the mid-eighteenth century by William Constable. The end result is an impressively large, brick-built mansion in a stylistic combination of Elizabethan and Georgian neo-Elizabethan. The main (east) front displays a fine coat of arms and a pretty pair of ogee-capped turrets; however, the real delights of the house lie inside.

William Constable provided the basis for

The west front of Burton Constable, around 1890.

its wonderful collection of furnishings, but later additions and the superb decoration were the work of Sir Thomas Aston Clifford-Constable (known as Sir Clifford) — who inherited the estate in 1823 — his first wife Marianne Chichester and her sister Eliza, and his second wife Rosina Brandon. This entertaining cast of characters had such an impact on the estate that it was almost bankrupt by the time of Sir Clifford's death in 1870.

Fortunately for the extravagant Sir Clifford, Lady Marianne brought with her a personal fortune; she and her husband travelled throughout Europe, buying furniture as they went, and also hired craftsmen from Hull and London to work in the house. So thrilled were Sir Clifford and his lady by the Oriental decor of the Brighton Pavilion, that they immediately installed a Chinese drawing room at Burton Constable, using a Chinese-wallpapered bedroom of 1783 as a basis. The new drawing room was equipped with much Chinese paraphernalia, including exquisitely venomous, carved golden dragons. The most striking room was converted by Marianne and Eliza Chichester from a coffee room, designed in 1773, to a family chapel, with red, deep blue and gold decoration almost everywhere.

Lady Marianne died in 1862, but her husband was already involved with Rosina Brandon, who became his second wife in 1865. She, too, was a great spendthrift, purchasing fashionable furnishings, but she eventually stripped the house of its contents in an attempt to profit from her liaison. Most were eventually returned, following a court case, in the early twentieth century. After a period of financial insecurity, and even the remote possibility of demolition, house and collection are now safe and available for all to see. It is a tremendous display of Yorkshire craftsmanship, as well as a monument to the urge to spend and the desire to collect.

The by-road which leads north from Sproatley on the B1238 and around Burton Constable to the A165 passes close to Wood Hall, an elegant Regency villa on the western edge of the estate. Built in 1820, its grey-brick, Picturesque design and round tower with low-pitched, conical roof are in the style of John Nash, but it was, perhaps, another London architect who added this touch of Italy to the wilds of Holderness.

Head south on the A165; the eventual destination is the medieval port of Hedon, but spare a moment for the enjoyably-named village of Swine, a mile along the by-road which runs west from Coniston. The church of St Mary is the attraction here; it originated as part of the church of a twelfth-century Cistercian nunnery, although much of the building dates from the later medieval period, and the tower was rebuilt in 1787. There are misericords on eight of the choir stalls, and another now resides in the pulpit.

Turn off the A165 just south of Coniston, and head south-east along a by-road to Bilton before joining the B1239 for Preston and ultimately Hedon, an early medieval port which declined in the face of competition from Hull.

The count of Aumale created the port and new town of Hedon around 1140, in order to take advantage of the profits available from river trade. Hedon, two miles inland, was linked with the Humber by a stream known as Hedon Haven, which had the small port of Paull at its mouth. Hedon grew on a rough grid pattern between the church of St Augustine and the Haven, which may have been artificially lengthened. But the town's period of prosperity was brief, just over a century; navigation along the shallow Haven was difficult, and by the late thirteenth century Hull was overtaking Hedon as a port. Nature had begun to take back the Haven by the early sixteenth century, and today there is little sign of the mooring basin at its end, which was closed in 1970 and then infilled.

Hedon now displays some good eighteenth-century building, while the church of St Augustine remains, sole survivor of the town's three parish churches, and an ample monument to medieval wealth. It was built on almost the same scale as Holy Trinity in Hull; here, the tower reaches 128 feet in height, while the length of the church is 165 feet. The chancel and crossing date from the late twelfth or early thirteenth century, while the nave is late thirteenth and mid-fourteenth century. The fine, Perpendicular tower was finished

The Church of St Augustine at Hedon. To the left is the south transept; its rose window was added by G E Street during the restoration of 1867-76.

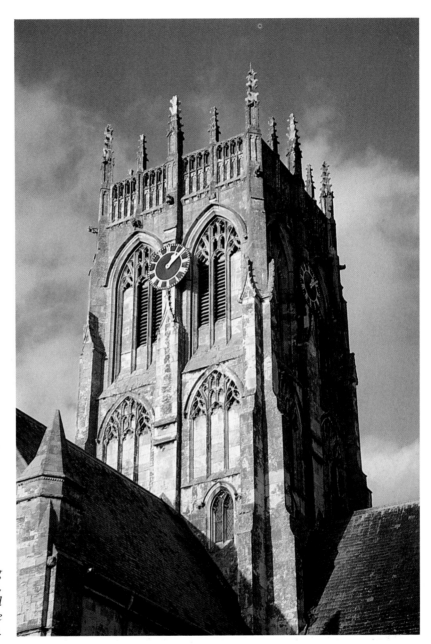

The Perpendicular crossing tower of St Augustine, Hedon, reaches a height of 128 feet and was completed during the 1430s.

during the 1430s. G E Street's restoration of 1867-76 added a rose window to the end wall of the south transept. The interior offers much evidence of a confused building history, and there is a good fourteenth-century font, octagonal with lavish decoration, but the power of St Augustine lies in its imposing exterior, a forceful reminder of Hedon's prosperous past.

From Market Place, almost beside the church, St Augustine's Gate leads south to the A1033, and continues as Sheriff Highway, crossing the old haven before reaching the Humber at Paull. The village was a minor pleasure resort for the people of Hull as early as 1808, and was popular with Sunday trippers in the Edwardian era.

At the water's edge, beside the old lighthouse, there is an expansive view over the estuary; ten miles distant to the west is the Humber Bridge, while the Lincolnshire Wolds stretch away to the south. Trinity House of Hull built the lighthouse in 1836, to replace earlier beacons. It became redundant in 1870, when two lights were erected about a mile to the south, and now functions as a particularly pleasing house. The domed, conical lighthouse, attached to a cottage, is three storeys high, with an iron balcony at top floor level.

A path leads along the estuary towards the new lights, and on rising ground just inland stands a gun battery, originally built in 1542. It was rebuilt in 1807 and greatly enlarged in 1861-4, when nineteen guns were sited on the elongated, pentagonal complex, which was in use until at least the Second World War.

The by-road north of the battery connects Paull with the A1033 at Thorngumbald, passing the remains of a fifteenth-century towered manor house at Paull Holme, where the road bends sharply left. Turn right at the main road, heading towards Patrington; at Ottringham, turn north along a by-road to reach Halsham, the medieval seat of the Constable family.

The Constables were lords of the manor of Halsham between the thirteenth century and its sale in 1873. Their home, until the move to Burton Constable in the late fifteenth century, was a manor house which stood at the far end of the village, just north of All Saints Church (turn left at the junction with the B1362). By the 1570s the manor house was a ruin, but the Constable family still took an interest in Halsham; the nearby school and almshouse, brick-built with a stepped gable, was founded by a bequest from Sir John Constable in 1579.

The most concrete evidence of their attachment to the village is the most unusual structure which stands across the road from the church: the Constable mausoleum. An avenue of yews leads to this circular, domed temple, built by Edward Constable in 1794-1802 as requested in the will of William Constable, who died in 1791. The design was the last work of Thomas Atkinson of York, who had been employed by William Constable during the 1770s. The external stonework carries only the slightest of Classical embellishments, while the top-lit interior is focussed on a pedestal bearing a white urn. In life, Constable and Atkinson built at Burton Constable in a style which harked back to the Elizabethan; but in death, all was cool Classicism.

Now for a return to the coast; head east along the B1362 to Withernsea, a putative Victorian seaside resort which lacked

The tapering, octagonal tower of the lighthouse rises above Withernsea in the 1920s. The lighthouse was built in 1892-4 — the walls are about five feet thick — and was in use until June 1976.

sufficient scenery and entertainment. The original village of Withernsea was lost to the waves in medieval times, and even by 1851 the population of its replacement was only 109. Promotion of the village as a resort began in 1852, when Hull businessman Anthony Bannister suggested building a railway which would carry agricultural produce from Holderness and take visitors to the coast. Withernsea was selected as the end point for the line, which was opened by the Hull & Holderness Railway Company on the 26th June 1854. Bannister became chairman of the railway, which invested in the tiny resort, buying bathing machines, laying out streets and, most importantly, building the Queens Hotel.

The hotel was designed by Cuthbert Brodrick in a quiet, Italianate style, and also opened in June 1854. Although 60,000 passengers used the railway in its first four months, the resort failed to develop significantly, and the North Eastern Railway took over the line in 1862. In the same year, the verdict given by a Yorkshire guidebook was that 'There is nothing to attract the visitor to Withernsea except the sea'. And that is no attraction at a seaside resort.

However, Bannister persisted with his forlorn attempts at development, setting up an improvement company in 1870, which indeed built a pier in 1877. Even this was not a success; its original length was 1,196 feet, but damage from storms and shipping reduced it to a pathetic fifty feet within twenty years. In addition, the Queens Hotel was closed in 1892. Surprisingly, the railway lasted until 1965.

Some traces remain of Withernsea's frustrated efforts to become a Scarborough, or at least a Filey. The grey-brick Queens Hotel became a hospital, while at the end of Pier Road, which connected station and hotel to the beach, is the castellated entrance to the non-existent pier. Then there are pleasant promenades, as well as some twentieth-century entertainments, but Withernsea's best building must be its elegant, white lighthouse. The tapering, octagonal tower stands a little inland, on Hull Road, and was erected in 1892-4 by Trinity House of Deptford. Although it ceased to function as a light in 1976, it still remains in use as a museum, and the 120 foot high tower provides excellent views over the Holderness coast.

Head back past the light, and about a mile and a half along the B1362, to take a small by-road which runs south on a meandering route to the village of Winestead, just off the A1033. The manor of Winestead was owned by the Hildyard family during the fifteenth to late nineteenth centuries; initially, their home was a moated manor house just west of the church, but in 1579 Sir Christopher Hildyard built a castellated mansion, known as Winestead Hall, a mile to the north. This was rebuilt in 1720, but demolished in 1936; the site, which retains its original stable block, is now occupied by a hospital.

The Maister family, Hull merchants, also owned property in Winestead. Old Park, part of the grounds of the medieval manor house lying to the west of the church, had been in their family since about 1700. There, in 1814, Arthur Maister began to build Winestead House, later known as White Hall, because of its grey brick. The hall — a fine, Greek Revival composition — was still under construction in 1824.

Winestead Church, St German, dates mainly from the fourteenth and fifteenth centuries, although the south chapel was built as a family shrine by Sir Christopher Hildyard in the early seventeenth century. There are, of course, several Hildyard monuments, including a substantial tomb-chest upon which the deceased lies at prayer, cushioned by the seventeenth-century version of a back-packer's sleeping mat.

The astonishing spire of Patrington Church now beckons eastward. It rises 189 feet above the flat Holderness plain, which seems to accentuate its height; it is visible for miles around. A church existed on the site of St Patrick in the twelfth century, but the present building dates from an intense period of construction during the late thirteenth to mid-fourteenth centuries. Later work, after a pause occasioned by the Black Death, included the spire, which rises from an unusual octagonal screen seated on the tower.

At first sight, the erection of such a large church — 150 feet in length — in a small, isolated village represents something of a puzzle. However, prestige played its part, as the Archbishop of York was lord of Patrington between the eleventh and sixteenth centuries, as did local economics and the ever-changing Humber Estuary. Although the village lay some distance from the Humber in the early medieval period, by the fourteenth century the silted lowlands had vanished under the water, leaving Patrington just over a mile from the river. A port developed at Patrington Haven, and the combination of sea trade with agricultural improvement in Holderness saw Patrington become an increasingly prosperous market centre.

The river began to change course again in the seventeenth century, and although Patrington Haven managed to continue its maritime role until the nineteenth century, silting has left Patrington and the river separated by three to four miles; this watery lowland area south-west of the village is known as Sunk Island. The village was left as solely an agricultural centre for the south of Holderness, with the usual allied trades such as milling, malting and brickmaking. The church of St Patrick, its architecture all of a piece, is a monument to the medieval good times; the Humber, first hero then villain, may be seen from its churchyard.

To explore Sunk Island, take the by-road which leads south-west from the village to Patrington Haven; there is little sign now of its past, as most of the warehouses have disappeared and the haven itself was filled in around 1970. Carry on, crossing Winestead Drain and ignoring a by-road to the left, and turn left at a T-junction to reach Holy Trinity Church, the centre of remote Sunk Island, marooned in the flattest of landscapes near the huge estuary.

In the sixteenth century it was an island visible only at low tide, but silting caused such growth that by the late seventeenth century it was felt to be worth reclaiming; a house was built on the new land soon after 1669, and was followed by a chapel and a few houses. After further reclamation around 1800, over a dozen farmhouses and a new chapel — which later became the parish church — were built.

As virgin land, Sunk Island was the property of the Crown, and the most distinctive remaining structures are those erected for the Crown estate during the 1850s and 1860s, after the initial leases had expired and the Crown began to take a more direct interest in the future of the island. The architect was Samuel Sanders Teulon, a favourite of Prince Albert and specialist in estate cottages and associated buildings, as well as a highly individual designer of churches. Teulon's work on the island comprised over thirty farms and cottages, mostly dated 1855 and using a dark, red brick; some show the initials of Victoria and Albert, and a crown. His school and school house followed in 1857, but his proposed church was never built. The original church was eventually demolished, to be replaced by the present Holy Trinity, designed by Teulon's close friend Ewan Christian, in 1876-7.

Head east from the church, across vast fields split by deep dikes, turning north at East Bank Farm then right at the T-junction, and so return to Patrington. From the village, the B1445 runs towards the coast, depositing the traveller at the top of another geographically variable obscurity, the Spurn Head peninsula.

First, though, a brief interlude at Welwick, only a couple of miles south-east of Patrington on the B1445. The apparently unspectacular church of St Mary, which dates from the thirteenth to fifteenth centuries, is entered through a disconcerting, two-storey brick porch, probably rebuilt in the eighteenth century. Inside, in the south aisle, may be found the gorgeously decorative remains of a monument to a priest, perhaps William de la Mare, provost of Beverley in 1338-60. Its heavily-carved canopy, with oodles of intricate detailing, once stretched completely across the window above and possibly right up to the roof. Its partial destruction is sad, but the effect is still quite splendid.

Onwards to the sea coast at Easington, where an excellent fourteenth or fifteenth century timber-framed tithe barn stands just south-west of All Saints Church. The thatched barn was built for Meaux Abbey, then owners of the church, and was part of Rectory Farm. It is probably the only remaining medieval farm building in the East Riding. Take the coast road south from Easington, which crosses Long Bank after about a mile and a half. This raised bank was constructed from the seventeenth to eighteenth centuries in order to protect the village from both sea and Humber, and runs on a southerly curve between the two, following the line of the parish boundary between Easington and Kilnsea, further to the south.

Near a southerly extension of the bank, about a third of a mile east of Long Bank Bridge, stands a strange, concrete object, a sixteen-foot high slab with a concave face looking to the east. The coast is less than half a mile away, which may give some clue as to its function, as may the battered remains of military activities on the peninsula. In fact, the miniature modern megalith is a sound mirror, built during or possibly soon after the First World War to detect airship or other airborne attacks. A chain of such mirrors existed on the coast from Hampshire and Kent to Yorkshire and Northumberland, although few remain; two more extant examples are sited in the North Riding, near Saltburn. The Kilnsea mirror still retains its microphone mounting, in front of the mirror, and there is also a tunnel leading to the cliff edge; the latter may have been connected with a nearby gun position.

Head south from Long Bank to Kilnsea, which sits on the inner edge of the peninsula. The original Kilnsea village, about half a mile to the east, was washed away in the early nineteenth century. A sand spit existed at Spurn in the seventh century, but was destroyed in the eleventh century; the cycle of creation and destruction occurred thrice more, the spit being breached in the fourteenth, seventeenth and nineteenth centuries, while being pushed steadily westward by the eroding power of the waves. The cycle, which seems to take around 250 years, has only been halted — temporarily, perhaps — by sea defence works on the Holderness coast.

The road continues east from Kilnsea, then turns south down the ever more bleak peninsula. It is just over three miles to Spurn Head itself, but within a mile, as the spit narrows, is the most easterly point in Yorkshire. What a weird spot this is: Humber to the west, North Sea to the east, and nothing but a vulnerable strip of shingle to connect the traveller with reality. In the distance, the craggy form of Bull Sand Fort, the final building in Holderness, can be seen far ahead in the estuary. The fort was built and armed in the First World War, and manned again during the Second World War.

The journey to the exposed headland ends with a fine piece of architecture, the lighthouse erected in 1895 by Trinity House. The earliest light on the headland dates from as early as 1427, while high and low lights — seen in vertical alignment by mariners following the safe shipping channel — were erected there in 1674. Coal for the lights was delivered to the beach by Newcastle upon Tyne colliers, an expensive process. Erosion forced changes in the positioning of the low light, but the high light survived until well after 1771, when work began on the construction of two new lights by Trinity House of Hull and Deptford. At first these were simply

The lighthouses of Spurn Head. On the left is the present light, built by Trinity House in 1895 and now completely automatic; to the right, in the Humber Estuary, is the stump of John Smeaton's low light, which was erected in 1776.

baskets, loaded with coals, which could be swung into the air on long levers; the designer was John Smeaton, who built the third Eddystone lighthouse. One light even ran along a type of railway track, so that it could be moved to mirror the direction of the shifting channel.

These lights were only temporary, and were soon replaced in 1776 by two brick towers, ninety and fifty feet in height, again designed by Smeaton and aligned so as to guide shipping down the Humber to Spurn Head. Illumination was again by coal, kept at white heat in specially-designed grates; oil lamps replaced this system in 1819. The low light was rebuilt in 1852, but went out of use when a new high light, the present 120 foot tower, was erected in 1895 to the design of Sir Thomas Matthews, engineer-in-chief to Trinity House.

The stump of the old low light still stands, to the west of the present lighthouse. The old high light was demolished but its circular compound, and the lightkeepers' houses, remain near the head of the peninsula. No keepers now, however, as the modern light was converted to automatic working in 1957.

The three-striped tower of Spurn Head lighthouse, a fine building in an amazing and thought-provoking setting, brings to an end this three-volume architectural odyssey around the Ridings of Yorkshire. It began with the cultivated resort of Harrogate and finishes on a windswept spit almost in the North Sea; it has taken in Romans and Regency, the polite and the rude, buildings vast and details tiny. The only certainty about Yorkshire's dramatic and daunting architectural heritage is that there is always more to see and enjoy; another building, another architect, another puzzle. So back to Harrogate, perhaps?

Glossary of Architectural Terms

almshouse A house or houses built and endowed by a charity for the relief of specific groups of people, often the poor or aged.

apse Semicircular end to a building, normally a chancel or chapel.

arcade Series of arches supported by columns; may be free-standing or attached to a building. Also a covered way lined with shops.

arch Load-bearing structure with its centre at a higher level than its sides, and supported by the mutual pressure of its building elements, often brick or stone.

Art Deco Popular interwar style which took the place of Art Nouveau *(qv)*; characterised by geometric forms and bold colour. Its name originated from a 1925 Paris exhibition of decorative arts.

Art Nouveau Style at its height around 1900, which appeared in the mid-1880s and lasted until the first decade of the twentieth century. Its hallmarks were flowing, organic forms and curving lines.

Arts and Crafts Late Victorian movement emphasising craft skills, exemplified by the work of William Morris & Co. Its decorative motifs were often derived from natural objects, while in architecture it featured new uses of vernacular *(qv)* forms.

ashlar Blocks of stone cut with square edges, finished smoothly and laid in even courses.

attached column Column which is not completely free-standing, but linked with a wall to the rear.

bailey Open area of a castle.

ball finial Finial *(qv)* in the shape of a globe.

balustrade A series of posts supporting a rail.

baptistery A building containing a font, where baptisms take place; may be part of a church, or completely separate.

bargeboard A protective wooden plank attached to the inclined gable *(qv)* ends of a building, often carved decoratively.

Baroque Late seventeenth and early eighteenth century architectural style, using massive, complex, curving forms in bold fashion.

barrel vault Vault *(qv)* with a semicircular cross-section.

bastion A projection at the corner of a fortification, often a turret or tower.

battered Wall with an inclined slope.

battlements The alternately raised and lowered upper edge of a parapet wall, often a castle wall.

bay Section of a building defined by fenestration *(qv)*.

beakhead Norman *(qv)* decorative motif resembling a row of bird-heads with projecting beaks. *(See also zigzag.)*

bellcote   Small frame on the roof of a building, usually a church, from which bells are hung.

belvedere   Summer-house *(qv)* with a view, often sited on a hill in a park. Also a viewing tower or turret on top of a house.

blank arch   An arched building element, with an infilled area (rather than a void) beneath the arch itself.

bow   Curved, and usually mainly glazed, projection from the wall of a building.

box pew   Georgian *(qv)* church bench enclosed by high, wooden panels and having a small door.

breastshot   Waterwheel in which water is fed on to the wheel at its vertical mid-point. *(See also overshot, pitchback and undershot.)*

Bronze Age   British era following the Stone Age and running from around 2100 BC to 700 BC. Marked by the use of bronze for tools, and the construction of stone circles.

buttress   Massive element of brickwork or stonework projecting from a wall and supporting the structure.

canted   An oblique corner, often used of bay windows with a non-rectangular section.

campanile   Bell tower separate from its parent building; also used to describe isolated chimneys.

capital head   The uppermost part of a column, often decorated.

castellated   Having turrets and battlements *(qv)*, as in a castle.

chancel   Area forming the east end of a church; the main altar is placed in the chancel, which is reserved for clergy and choir.

chancel arch   Church archway at the west end of the chancel, normally dividing the nave from the chancel.

chantry chapel   Chapel endowed to celebrate masses as ordered by its founder.

chapel of ease   Chapel built to enable members of a congregation living distant from the parish church to attend serices locally.

chapter house   Part of the eastern range *(qv)* of monastic buildings next to the cloister, often circular or polygonal in plan. It was used by the monks for discussion of all types of monastic business.

choir   In a church, the section of the chancel where service is sung.

Classical   Various forms of Classical style dominated English architecture from the early seventeenth century until the early nineteenth century. It was originally inspired by Greek and Roman architecture, and then by Renaissance interpretations of past styles. Classical buildings featured traditionally correct proportions and severely-restrained decoration.

clerestory   Uppermost part of the main walls of a building, with a series of windows; a term often used in church architecture to describe a nave with windows in its upper storey.

colonnade   Linked series of columns.

conceit   Fanciful element.

Corinthian   Order of Classical *(qv)* architecture involving specified proportions of column and capital, with elaborate foliage decoration of the latter.

crenellate   Crenellations are also known as battlements *(qv)*; a crenellated wall has alternating higher and lower sections along its upper edge.

crocket   Decorative element, often carved in leaf shapes, which appears on Gothic *(qv)* spires, gables *(qv)* and other pre-eminent features.

crossing tower   Church tower sited above

the area where the nave, chancel and transepts intersect.

cupola   A dome; usually used to describe a small dome crowning a roof.

curtain wall   Originally the outer wall of a castle, connecting its towers, but now also applied to any external non-load-bearing wall.

dado   Decorative finish of the lower part (to about waist height) of an internal wall.

Decorated   See Gothic.

diaper   Repetitive decorative motif, often in pattern of squares or, most frequently, lozenges.

Doric   Order of Classical *(qv)* architecture involving specified proportions of column and capital, with very little decoration of the latter.

Early English   See Gothic.

Edwardian   Building design in the first decade of the twentieth century encompassed a range of styles from severe Classical to highly-decorative Edwardian Baroque. These may perhaps all be characterised by a preoccupation with novel interpretations of existing styles, and the search for a new and British architecture. The resulting buildings differed widely in appearance but shared a certain confidence.

Egyptian Revival   The use of motifs, such as obelisks *(qv)* and pyramids, derived from ancient Egyptian architecture. The early nineteenth century and the 1920s are the two most recent revivals, the latter resulting from the discovery in 1922 of the tomb of Tutankhamun.

Elizabethan   Style of the late sixteenth and early seventeenth centuries typified by symmetrical façades, large, mullioned *(qv)* and transomed *(qv)* windows, and decorative strapwork *(qv)*.

encaustic tile   Clay tile of the Victorian period, used mainly as flooring, with decoration originally based on medieval tile designs. Later Victorian examples featured colourful geometric decoration, and were widely used in public buildings as well as churches.

eyecatcher   Building, normally in a park or garden, erected to enhance the view.

façade   The external front of a building.

faience   Inclusive term for all ceramic materials used in an architectural context, such as on a faience façade.

fenestration   The pattern of windows in the wall of a building.

finial   Decorative feature of varying form found on top of spires, gables *(qv)* and other tall architectural elements; originally Gothic *(qv)*.

fluted   Decorative vertical grooves on, for example, a column; grooves are shallow and concave.

flying buttress   Buttress *(qv)* with lower part detached from building it supports.

folly   Building with no purpose, at least in terms of normal cost-benefit criteria. Follies are often decorative, with eccentric architectural features, and frequently appear as park ornaments.

gable   Triangular upper part of a wall defined by a pitched roof. Variants include the Dutch gable, which has curved sides and is topped by a pediment *(qv)*.

gallery   A partial upper floor, overlooking the main internal space of a building; specifically in a church, an upper floor above an aisle.

Georgian   Architectural style of the early eighteenth to early nineteenth centuries, with plain, Classical *(qv)* exteriors and more decorative interiors, culminating in those of Robert Adam in the late eighteenth century.

Germano-Gothic   Victorian style in which Gothic (*qv*) is tempered by traditional German elements, particularly turrets, gables (*qv*) and steeply-pitched roofs with small dormer windows.

Gothic   Style featuring pointed arches (*qv*), arcading (*qv*) and flying buttresses (*qv*); together they formed a structural system which minimised wall area. It was introduced to Britain in the early twelfth century, becoming known as the Early English style. This developed into the Decorated style, with more prominent decoration and tracery (*qv*), in the late thirteenth century. By the second half of the fourteenth century the Perpendicular (*qv*) style, with the emphasis on straight, vertical elements, had come to the fore and lasted for around 250 years. The Victorian Gothic Revival was particularly important for church architecture.

Gothick   Style of the Gothic (*qv*) Revival of the mid-eighteenth century, which was first applied to pleasure buildings and featured frilly, highly-decorative Gothic motifs.

Greek Doric   See Order.

Greek Revival   The fashion for building in a style similar to ancient Greek architecture, which began in the 1780s and reached its peak in the 1820s and 1830s.

hammerbeam roof   Roof structure formed by a series of roof supports or hammer-posts projecting vertically upward from brackets or hammerbeams set in the top of the wall.

High Victorian   Architecture of the mid-nineteenth century, often featuring polychromy (*qv*) and the use of varied building materials.

ice-house   Garden outbuilding popular in the eighteenth and nineteenth centuries, often built with country houses; its purpose was to store ice. Frequently built partly underground, and with a roughly egg-shaped internal space.

Ionic   Order of Classical (*qv*) architecture involving specified proportions of column and capital, with twin spiral-pattern decoration of the latter.

Iron Age   Period from around 700 BC until the time of the Roman invasion; iron was used for tools and weapons.

Italianate   Victorian style which involved Italian Renaissance elements such as low-pitched (*qv*) roofs, towers and round-headed windows.

Jacobean   Style of the early seventeenth century, a development of the Elizabethan (*qv*); important elements were large windows, extravagant decoration and dominant gables (*qv*).

Jacobethan   Victorian or Edwardian style combining elements traditionally found in Jacobean (*qv*) and Elizabethan (*qv*) buildings, such as mullioned (*qv*) windows, a high level of decoration and prominent gables (*qv*).

Jesse window   Stained glass window showing a genealogical tree of Christ's descent from the root of Jesse, the father of David.

king post   Central, vertical timber supporting a pitched roof, and rising from a beam connecting the tops of the walls to the ridge of the roof.

lancet window   Narrow, pointed-arched window.

lychgate   Covered gateway at the entrance to a churchyard; originally provided a resting place for a coffin.

mansard roof   Pitched roof with two differently-sloping sections on each side: a steeper section rising from the wall, followed by a lower-pitched section reaching to the ridge.

medieval   The era between the fifth and fifteenth centuries, from when the Romans left Britain to the coming of the Renaissance. In architectural terms, it encompasses Saxon *(qv)*, Norman *(qv)*, Romanesque *(qv)* and Gothic *(qv)* periods.

misericord   Bracket, often decoratively carved, on the underside of a hinged choir-stall or seat; when the stall was raised, the misericord supported the standing chorister.

Moorish   Stylistic features used in the late Victorian period and taken from the ancient Islamic architecture of Spain and North Africa; its main forms are elaborate domes and arcades.

mullion   Vertical element separating sections of a window.

nave   Area forming the west end of a church, which may be extended to the north or south with aisles.

navigation   A canal, often including one or more sections of improved river passage.

Norman   Architecture of the period from the early eleventh to the mid-twelfth centuries. Its main features are massive structures, round-headed arches and geometrical ornament.

obelisk   Tall, upright column, usually with a square cross-section and tapering towards the top.

ogee   Double curve, of concave and convex elements.

openwork   Describes a structure, often decorative, comprising interconnected building members; the network forms a pattern with spaces between the members. It may be a hollow structure, or take two-dimensional form.

order   In Classical *(qv)* architecture, describes the combination of base, column, capital (at the head of the column) and entablature (the latter refers to the section of building immediately above the capital). The traditional orders include Tuscan — the simplest, with a plain column — and Greek Doric, where the column is fluted *(qv)* and baseless.

oriel   Bay window on an upper floor, unsupported at ground level, thus overhanging.

overshot   Waterwheel in which the water arrives at the top of the wheel, turning the wheel in the direction of the water flow. *(See also breastshot, pitchback and undershot.)*

palisade   A fence, normally constructed from wooden stakes.

Palladian   Classical *(qv)* style derived from the buildings of the sixteenth century Italian architect Andrea Palladio, which was introduced to England in the early seventeenth century. The style emphasises symmetry and ancient systems of proportion, and strongly features the colonnade *(qv)*, portico *(qv)* and venetian window *(qv)*.

parapet   Low wall protecting a sudden drop, for example at the side of a bridge or the top of a house.

pediment   Low-pitched gable *(qv)* above features such as a portico (qv), door or window.

pele tower   See tower house.

Perpendicular   Gothic *(qv)* style dominant between the late fourteenth century and the late sixteenth century, when the Elizabethan *(qv)* style became established. Perpendicular style strongly emphasised vertical architectural elements, as did the more decorative Elizabethan.

Picturesque   Mid-eighteenth to early nineteenth century style, largely used in the context of cottages, country houses and garden design, but having broader implications, and partly derived from the images of seventeenth-century landscape painting. The style was highly decorative, combining ruggedness with ruins, and used disparate elements such as Italianate *(qv)* motifs in an asymmetrical fashion. The object was to create a sublime vision by combining nature and architecture.

pier   Solid, load-bearing pillar, normally of stone. Also used to describe a jetty projecting from a land base into the sea.

pilaster   Column projecting only slightly from a wall.

pitch   The angle of slope of a roof.

pitchback   Waterwheel in which the water arrives at the top of the wheel, thus turning the wheel in the opposite direction to the water flow. *(See also breastshot, overshot and undershot.)*

polychromy   Decorated in many colours. Mid-Victorian architects produced polychromy not only by using paint, but by combining different building materials; this technique is known as structural polychromy.

porte cochere   A porch providing sufficient covered area for a carriage or other wheeled vehicle to pass beneath; sometimes found at railway stations or country houses.

portico   Entrance space of a building, often a house or church, which is covered but normally open to the sides, and has a pediment *(qv)* supported by columns; the whole is in the style of a temple.

prodigy house   Large-scale Elizabethan *(qv)* country house, with huge areas of glazing and abundant decoration; a prodigious building.

Queen Anne Revival   The architectural style used for small domestic buildings of the Queen Anne period (early eighteenth century) was revived in the late nineteenth century; in its revival form, it emphasised red-brick walls and contrasting white, wooden window frames.

range   A row of buildings.

Regency   Style predominant between the 1790s and the early 1840s; when used strictly, the term relates to the period 1811-20 when the future George IV was prince regent. This neo-Classical style made free use of ancient forms, resulting in eclectic versions of Classical *(qv)* structures, which sometimes verged on the Picturesque *(qv)*.

reredos   Screen or similar structure sited behind, and usually above, the altar; often decorated.

Rococo   The final stylistic phase of the Baroque *(qv)*, which occurred during the middle of the eighteenth century in England, where it was used only for interiors and garden buildings. The elaborately decorative Rococo style emphasised delicacy and lightness of form and colour, as opposed to the sombre heaviness of the Baroque.

Roman   Buildings of the Roman occupation of Britain, which lasted from around AD 43 to AD 409, and included sophisticated baths and temples.

Romanesque   Term used to describe the dominant architectural style of Europe from the tenth century (or before) until the eleventh century, and marked by the use of the round arch; roughly equivalent to the

Norman *(qv)* style in Britain. The round-arched Romanesque form also underwent a late Victorian revival.

rood loft The wooden rood or cross was usually erected at the east end of the nave *(qv)*, on a beam stretching across the upper part of the chancel arch *(qv)*. Just below it was the rood loft, a gallery which might itself carry the rood or other images; the loft also stretched across the chancel arch. Rood lofts were introduced in the fifteenth century.

rood screen Screen beneath the rood loft *(qv)*, separating the nave and chancel.

rose window Large, circular, church window, with tracery *(qv)* pattern radiating from its centre.

rotunda A room or building with a circular plan, and often with a domed roof. When used as a decorative garden building, the rotunda often has a colonnade *(qv)* in place of its solid wall.

rubblestone Unfinished stone in various shapes, with rough surfaces and few right-angled corners; irregular rubble may be worked into horizontal courses during building, in which case it is known as coursed rubblestone.

rustication Massive blocks of masonry which are separated by deep, V-shaped joints; often used on the lower part of the external walls of large buildings to add weight to the composition.

Saxon English architecture of the seventh to early eleventh centuries. Simple churches occurred in the seventh century, and towers first appeared in the tenth century; basic geometric decoration was often prominent.

Scottish Baronial Style originated by architect William Burn around 1830 for Scottish country houses, in which the basic building was adorned with large, circular towers and turrets, often capped by steeply-pitched, conical roofs; the whole was in the Scottish tradition of fortified architecture.

Second Empire Style current from the 1850s until the end of the nineteenth century; the main elements emphasised the height of the building: turrets, chimneys, domes and the mansard roof *(qv)*. The term arises from extensions to the Louvre made by Napoleon III, which used French Renaissance decorative forms.

solar The upper living-room of a medieval house.

spandrel Roughly triangular area between the tops of adjacent arches *(qv)* or arched windows; may be decorated.

strapwork Late sixteenth century decorative motif of intertwined bands.

stucco Smooth or decorative plasterwork on walls or ceilings.

summer-house Garden building, often decorative, used mainly in summer, for contemplation of the view and possibly as a residence.

tie beam Main horizontal beam in a roof structure, which connects the tops of opposing walls.

timber-framed Type of building construction in which an open, wooden framework, usually of horizontal and vertical timbers, forms the walls; this frame is then filled in with non-structural matter such as plaster.

tower house A medieval fortified house, of three storeys or more in height, most frequently found in Scotland and the north of England, where it is usually known as a pele tower.

tracery   Pattern of ribs defining the glazing of the upper section of a window; also used to describe the pattern of decoration on vaults *(qv)*.

transept   A section of a building running, at a right angle on the plan, across its main space; the transepts are the elements which protrude from its sides. They are most often found in church architecture, where the north and south transepts may form the arms of a cross-shaped church.

transom   Horizontal element separating sections of a window.

Tudor   Architecture of the sixteenth century, culminating in the Elizabethan *(qv)* period, when the professional architect came to prominence for the first time.

Tuscan   See order.

undercroft   A vaulted *(qv)* room, set below another room and sometimes underground.

undershot   Waterwheel in which the water passes along the lower edge of the wheel. *(See also breastshot, overshot and pitchback.)*

vault   Arched roof-structure, normally in brick or stone, with semicircular or more complex cross-section; a more complex vault is divided by a pattern of curved ribs.

venetian window   Window in three vertical sections, of which the central section is taller than the side sections and has a semicircular top.

vermiculated   Type of rustication *(qv)* in which the blocks of masonry are carved with intersecting, curving shapes having the appearance of worm tracks.

vernacular   The architecture of everyday buildings, with the emphasis on the use of locally-available materials, as opposed to the style of grander buildings designed by architects.

vestry   Small room, in which vestments are kept, attached to a church.

Victorian   Architecture of the reign of Queen Victoria, 1837-1901, sometimes extended to encompass the reign of William IV, 1830-37. A period of stylistic eclecticism in which Gothic *(qv)*, Classical *(qv)* and other styles all had their proponents, resulting in the building of varied, and often colourful, structures.

wing   An almost self-contained section of a building projecting to either side of its central mass.

winter garden   Conservatory-style structure, often built of cast iron and glass; popular in the domestic context on a small scale, and as large-scale entertainment buildings (particularly at resorts), from mid- to late nineteenth century.

zigzag   Norman *(qv)* decorative motif of a line turning sharply and alternately to right and left. *(See also beakhead.)*

Bibliography

The East Riding and its Architecture
K J Allison, *The East Riding of Yorkshire Landscape* (Hodder and Stoughton 1976).
M F Barbey, *Civil Engineering Heritage — Northern England* (Thomas Telford 1981).
Painton Cowen, *A Guide to Stained Glass in Britain* (Michael Joseph 1985).
Charles Hadfield, *The Canals of Yorkshire and North East England* Vols I and II (David and Charles 1972 and 1973).
Jane Hatcher, *The Industrial Architecture of Yorkshire* (Phillimore 1985).
Gwyn Headley and Wim Meulenkamp, *Follies* (Jonathan Cape 1990).
Peter Kent, *British Regional Geology: Eastern England from the Tees to the Wash* (HMSO 1980).
Nikolaus Pevsner, *Yorkshire: York and the East Riding* (Penguin 1972).

The Walled City
Alan Johnson, *The Inns and Alehouses of York* (Hutton Press 1989).
Hans van Lemmen, *Decorative Tiles and Architectural Ceramics in Yorkshire* (Tiles and Architectural Ceramics Society 1988).
Patrick Nuttgens, *York: Buildings in the City* (EP Publishing 1978).
Royal Commission on the Historical Monuments of England, *York — Historic Buildings in the Central Area* (HMSO 1981).
P M Tillott (ed), *Victoria History of Yorkshire — The City of York* (Oxford University Press 1961).
The Works in Architecture of John Carr (York Georgian Society 1973).
Treasurer's House (National Trust 1982).

York Without
Chris Brooks, *Mortal Remains* (Wheaton 1989).
Michael Hall, 'Eloquence of Line' (*Country Life*, 19th August 1993).
Hugh Murray, *This Garden of Death* (Friends of York Cemetery 1988).
Jack Simmons, *The Railway in Town and Country 1830-1914* (David and Charles 1986).
The Strays and Ways of York (Sessions Book Trust 1968).

Fens, Carrs and Commons

K J Allison (ed), *A History of the County of York, East Riding*, Volume III (Oxford University Press 1976).

Winifred Ann Los, 'From Brickyard to Builder's Yard: Brickmaking in East Yorkshire' (*Construction History Society Newsletter*, October 1991).

Arthur Oswald, 'Everingham Park, Yorkshire' (*Country Life*, 15th and 22nd February 1968).

A Heap of Mountains

Jill Allibone, *The Wallpaintings at Garton-on-the-Wolds* (Pevsner Memorial Trust 1991).

K J Allison (ed), *A History of the County of York, East Riding*, Volume IV (Oxford University Press 1979).

Colin Hayfield, *Thixendale Remembered* (Spring Hill Publications 1988).

John Hutchinson, *George Edmund Street in East Yorkshire* (University of Hull 1981).

Arthur Oswald, 'Hall Garth, Goodmanham, Yorkshire' (*Country Life*, 23rd February and 2nd March 1961).

John Popham, 'Sir Christopher Sykes at Sledmere' (*Country Life*, 16th and 23rd January 1986).

From Brigg to Bridlington

K J Allison (ed), *A History of the County of York, East Riding*, Volume II (Oxford University Press 1974).

Jonathan Brown, *Steeped in Tradition* (University of Reading 1983).

Mark Girouard, *Robert Smythson and the Elizabethan Country House* (Yale University Press 1983).

Douglas B Hague and Rosemary Christie, *Lighthouses: Their Architecture, History and Archaeology* (Gomer Press 1975).

Christopher Morris (ed), *The Illustrated Journeys of Celia Fiennes* (Macdonald 1982).

Sue Read, *Hello Campers!* (Bantam Press 1986).

Filey Town Walks (Filey District Civic Society c1982).

The Finest Fortification

K J Allison (ed), *A History of the County of York, East Riding*, Volumes I and VI (Oxford University Press 1969 and 1989).

A G Chamberlain, 'Mountain of Hull' (*Architectural Review*, October 1968).

Edward Gillett and Kenneth A MacMahon, *A History of Hull* (Oxford University Press 1980).

Elisabeth Hall (ed), *Michael Warton of Beverley* (University of Hull 1986).

Ivan and Elisabeth Hall, *Georgian Hull* (William Sessions 1978).

Ivan and Elisabeth Hall, *Historic Beverley* (Beverley Bookshop 1981).
Gordon Jackson, *Hull in the Eighteenth Century* (Oxford University Press 1972).
Christopher Ketchell and Jose Montgomery, *Tiles Tour of Hull* (Hull College of Further Education 1990).
Jim Low, 'Housing the People of Hull' (*Architects' Journal*, 14th July 1976).
Keith Miller, John Robinson, Barbara English and Ivan Hall, *Beverley: An Archaeological and Architectural Study* (HMSO 1982).
John H Rumsby, *The Hull Dock Offices 1787-1976* (City of Kingston upon Hull Museums & Art Galleries 1976).
'Looking at Hull' (*Architects' Journal*, 14th July 1976).

Nothing Remarkable?
K J Allison (ed), *A History of the County of York, East Riding*, Volume V (Oxford University Press 1984).
Barbara English, *The Lords of Holderness* (Oxford University Press 1979).
Ivan Hall, 'Burton Constable Hall, Yorkshire' (*Country Life*, 6th August 1992).
E W Sockett, 'Yorkshire's Early Warning System, 1916-1936' (*Yorkshire Archaeological Journal*, 1989).
Richard Woodman, *View From the Sea* (Century Publishing 1985).
'Hornsea Tower' (*Architectural Review*, May 1969).

Index

Main entries are in **bold**; illustrations in *italics*.